THE
PRAYER BOOK
OF
MICHELINO DA BESOZZO

THE
PRAYER BOOK
OF
MICHELINO DA BESOZZO

introduction by
COLIN EISLER

legends by
PATRICIA CORBETT
and
COLIN EISLER

The Pierpont Morgan Library, New York

GEORGE BRAZILLER
NEW YORK

Joyous Hours for Jane and Patrick

Reproduced from the Illuminated Manuscript (M 944) belonging to
The Pierpont Morgan Library in New York

Library of Congress Catalog Card Number: 81-68186
International Standard Book Number: 0-8076-1016-X

Printed in Switzerland by Imprimeries Réunies

Miniatures photographed by Charles Passela
Book design by Rita Grasso

CONTENTS

ACKNOWLEDGMENTS

M y very warmest thanks to William Voelkle, associate
curator of Medieval and Renaissance manuscripts at the
Pierpont Morgan Library, New York, for his great gener-
osity in placing his excellent analysis of Michelino's manuscript at my disposal. I am also indebted to Eliot Rowland
for an enlightening discussion of the prayer book.

C.E.

INTRODUCTION

In his introduction to the greatest gathering of Lombard art ever held, the dazzling *Arte Lombarda* exhibit of 1957, one of the twentieth century's most knowledgeable scholars of Italian art, Roberto Longhi, saved his highest praise for a work not included in the Milanese show. Writing of the prayer book then locked away in the library of Dr. Martin Bodmer in Switzerland, Professor Longhi characterized the manuscript as one of indescribable beauty and named the illuminator, Michelino da Besozzo, as the greatest painter of the International Style that flourished around 1400. With the generous assistance of Miss Alice Tully, this ravishing little book was bought in 1970 by the Pierpont Morgan Library in memory of Dr. Edward Graeffe.

Who was the prayer book's illuminator? Although little known today, Michelino enjoyed an immense reputation during his long, productive lifetime. Calling Michelino's art superior to that of all others, the humanist Umberto Decembrio praised the painter in his *De Republica*. The same scholar's son, Pier Candido, continued his praise of the master in his *Vita* of Giovanni Maria Visconti, describing Michelino's portrait of the tyrant (as cruel as he was ugly, assassinated in 1412) as evidence of the artist's great skill. A fifteenth-century chronicle, the *Codex Picenardiano,* groups the painter with the most splendid masters from antiquity to the writer's time. Michelino is named in company with Apelles and Parrhasius, Giotto, Jean d'Arbois, and Gentile de Fabriano. Lomazzo, the late sixteenth-century Vasari of Lombard painting, cites Michelino as the founder of the school of Milanese art and rates him as its greatest early master.

Although only works from the first quarter of the fifteenth century survive, Michelino is known to have been productive (he was especially celebrated as a portraitist) until 1449. Probably born about 1368, the young Michelino, described as an infant prodigy, seems to have been trained in the workshop of Giovannino de' Grassi, a brilliant manuscript illuminator, also active as sculptor and architect in the employ of Giangaleazzo Visconti II.

Son of Bianca da Savoia and husband of Isabelle de France (a sister of King Charles V), Giangaleazzo was a friend of Petrarch and a great patron of the arts. He undertook the development of the university at Pavia, built up his library at Pavia to rival those of his French relatives, and showed much admiration for Northern art. But Giangaleazzo had political ambitions as well. In 1385 he had his uncle, Bernabo Visconti, killed. With Bernabo out of the way, Giangaleazzo could now control Milan as well as Pavia and begin to consolidate his power in Italy. The next year saw work begin on the new cathedral of Milan. Vast numbers of French, Netherlandish, and German artists were brought to the city to help with the colossal project, which Giangaleazzo paid for out of his own pocket. In 1395 he sought to further enhance his power by the purchase of the title Duke of Milan from his brother-in-law, the Holy Roman Emperor Wenceslaus of Bohemia. Finally in 1396 work began on his tomb at the Certosa of Pavia, which was modelled on the recently established Burgundian ducal burial site at the newly founded Carthusian monastery near Dijon. Thus Giangaleazzo copied Northern style for death as well as life.

During the years when Giangaleazzo's armies threatened to take over all Italy, Michelino received his first major commissions for frescoes and altarpieces in the churches of Pavia.

Although most of the master's wall paintings dating from 1388 onward are destroyed, one of the few to survive is a powerful *Crucifixion* in the Chapel of the Eremo near Crevenna.

Landscape, the setting of life's time and tide, was shown with remarkable care and innovation in Northern Italy. New approaches to nature are found in the lavishly illustrated guides to healthy life, the *Tacuinum Sanitatis,* and the splendid plant studies, such as the *Carrara Herbal*, all of which reflect a scrutiny and a sense of time and place hithertofore unknown in postclassical art. Manuscript illuminators of the period, including Anovelo da Imbonate and Pietro da Pavia who worked at Giangaleazzo's court, showed a vital, imaginative use of floral borders and floral motifs against gold backgrounds that impressed the young Michelino. A Book of Hours he prepared for use in Pavia (Avignon, Bibliothèque Municipale, Ms. 111) has calendrical scenes of the labors of the months that show the artist's response to the growing interest in genre scenes. His workshop illustrated Boccaccio's treatise on landscape in a manuscript dated 1401 (Copenhagen, Royal Library, Cat. No. 2092), which reveals a similar concern for exploring nature and a sympathy for its forms.

At the very end of the century, in 1399, the most brilliant northern manuscript illuminator, the Bruges master Jacques Coene, worked in Milan for the Visconti. Long known as the Boucicaut Master, this artist may have contributed to Michelino's apprehension of light and space. Northern influence must be responsible for the effect of transcendent illumination that makes the young master's pages windows of ineffable beauty.

The first of Michelino's few securely dated works is a large illumination for the *Eulogy of Giangaleazzo Visconti,* written by Pietro de Castelleto and completed by January 26, 1403 (Paris, Bibliothèque Nationale, Ms. Lat. 5888). The recently deceased duke is shown as he is received into heaven and crowned as Count of Virtue by a nude, plump infant Jesus seated on the Virgin's lap. This noble title had already been conferred upon Giangaleazzo in life as part of his first wife's dowry. But here he is shown in Paradise, enjoying the domain of virtue in a moral rather than territorial sense, surrounded by personifications of the Virtues who resemble many of the female saints in the Morgan Library's prayer book. Energetic borders bristle with floral imagery and prophets' heads. A Burgundian-style depiction of this eulogy's author, shown just below, reveals Michelino's celebrated skills as a portraitist.

A series of medallions in the same manuscript trace the Visconti lineage back to its putative origins, the marriage of King Anchises of Troy to Venus, with Jupiter conducting the ceremony. The wedding ring, unique in design, has a large flower floating on top of the circlet. This motif reappears, although in a slightly more modest version, in the ring given by Joseph to Mary in the *Marriage of the Virgin* (New York, Metropolitan Museum of Art). Only one other panel painting by Michelino is known, *The Mystical Marriage of Saint Catherine* (Siena, Pinacoteca). Again, the ring appears. Such love for distinctive gold work, truly *bijou de fantaisie* (the French for costume jewelry), suggests that the painter, like so many leading masters of the time—Ghiberti, Brunelleschi, the Limbourg brothers—began his career as a goldsmith. The International Style, after all, shares many of the glittering qualities of the goldsmith's craft.

Designing, carving, and polychroming sculpture, as well as planning and making stained glass, were among the Lombard artist's many other skills. His work on the vast new cathedral of Milan is recorded over a long time span; the church's archives describe Michelino as "supreme master painter and master of stained glass" as late as 1420. Among the myriad activities in which he was engaged was the decoration of the Chapel of Saints Quirico and Giulitta, for which he painted an altarpiece, made and polychromed sculpture, and prepared and executed the stained glass.

By moving from medium to medium, shifting from work in metal and glass to panel and fresco painting and manuscript illumination, Michelino built up a richly varied technical vocabulary. A unique quality of light, a rich fusion of the decorative and the observed, a keen and witty touch and the artist's swift and probing vision inform all his works. A single, tantalizing reference suggests that Michelino was also active as an architect, the profession of his presumed teacher, Giovannino de' Grassi. Indeed, Michelino's genius for conveying light points to some practical experience as a Gothic architect familiar with the sight of walls dissolved through webs of stained glass.

Despite its extravagant consumerism, as conspicuous in heaven as it was rampant on earth, the period of the International Style was also an age of studied innocence. Guileless juvenile faces and lithe figures abound. The Christians of the late Middle Ages chose to depict ancient and biblical subjects but portrayed themselves as elegant youths, hoping thereby to blot the recent horrors of the Black Death, the devastation, the hunger, the disease of the past half-century. Escapist and materialistic at the same time, this was a style, and a world view, that went well with the despotic nature of the Visconti and other Northern Italian courts. These tyrannical princes patronized Petrarch and paid elaborate lip service to classical antiquity, and they wanted an art that in its precious grace lent substance to their claims of ancient lineage. This was also a time when, almost two centuries after St. Francis of Assisi, the reassuring joys of

Christ's infancy were again appreciated. In Christian faith and art the immortal soul was seen as an infant, born for love, counting on care.

Typical of Michelino's rare gift of combining contrasting elements—the warm and the courtly, the divine and the intimate—is his painting of the *Mystical Marriage of Saint Catherine* (Siena, Pinacoteca). Here the artist's name, with those of Saints Anthony and John the Baptist, and all the flower-embellished crowns and halos are built up in *pastiglia*, raised and gilded gesso. Shown as a shy, little girl, Princess Catherine kneels awestruck at the side of the throne, her royal crimson and ermine train kicked before her; this rich drapery lies before the throne, forming a great calligraphic volute.

Mary, resembling a long-necked northern ivory carving, places one hand on Catherine's back while supporting the Christ child, who curls his toes and parts petulantly with his ring. The bluff, almost Byzantine-looking saints witness the mystical marriage. A small black pig, engagingly *en suite* under the dark profile of his master, Saint Antony, raises his snout in celebratory fashion, a tribute to Michelino's gifts as *animalier* and to Anthony Abbot's humanity.

Michelino's continued activity as a painter of frescoes and altarpieces and as a maker of stained glass and statuary was punctuated through the 1420s by the creation of illuminated manuscripts. By 1410 patronage had brought him beyond Milan and Pavia. While working in Venice he was interviewed by Giovanni Alcherio, the agent of the Duc de Berry, who praised him as "the most excellent painter among all the painters in the world." Such glowing words may explain the influence that Michelino, as Pächt has shown, had on the Limbourg brothers, the brilliant young illuminators at the Duc de Berry's court, as well as Michelino's important contribution to Venetian painting.

Alcherio recorded Michelino's formula for working with azurite in a "recipe" book of manuscript illuminators' and calligraphers' techniques now in the Bibliothèque Nationale. In 1414 Michelino illuminated a beautiful page of the *Letters of Saint Jerome* for the Cornaro (Corner) family, one of the wealthiest in Venice. This work shows a fluency unmatched in the manuscripts mentioned previously, and a new Gothic gracefulness. Three quatrefoils contain the *Nativity; God the Father Holding the Dead, Crucified Son;* and the *Resurrection.* Each scene is confined within geometrical forms that seem to grow from the blue and green flowered border—it is as if nature rather than art had devised their contours.

Only one other book-like work of Michelino's is known, the so-called *Libretto degli Anacoretti* or *Little Book of the Anchorites,* which was drawn around 1404 (Rome, Gabinetto Nazionale delle Stampe). Not devoted to any single theme, although it does include scenes of monks living in the wilderness and episodes from the life of Saint Anthony Abbott, the *libretto* is really a notebook. In format it is comparable to the celebrated volume of Giovannino de' Grassi at Bergamo, which is filled with genre subjects and animal studies. Heightened with white, Michelino's drawings in this collection also include scenes of elegant life and designs for elaborate fountains and other like commissions that an artist attached to a court might undertake.

As late as 1449, Michelino was promoted by the Venetian humanist Marcello as "the Polykleites of our times." These flattering words appeared in a letter sent to the wife of King René of Anjou, the amateur painter and keen collector and patron of Italian art, to accompany a gift of playing cards painted by Michelino. The painter is also known to have made frescoes for the Borromeo family, bankers to the Visconti, who had provided Michelino with colors from

Northern Europe. Michelino's vibrant art may even have influenced the Venetian use of color, providing a point of departure for that school's Renaissance ideal.

❧❧

Ninety-five vellum leaves in length, the Morgan Library's little prayer book measures 6¾ inches in height by 4¾ inches in width. The manuscript now has twenty-two full-page illuminations, each with a facing prayer page. Both pages have a similar flowered border. There is also one historiated initial. The borders on the miniature pages are known to be by Michelino, but some of those on the prayer pages may have been painted by an assistant, who may also be responsible for several illuminations of standing saints. Twenty-five additional prayer pages have lost their facing illumination pages. The entire text was written by a single scribe.

All the book's prayers are arranged according to the liturgy, dedicated to the feasts and the saints of the church calendar. It opens with the Nativity, which faces the prayer for Christmas Day. The book's last image is that of Saint Lucy *(fol. 89v)*, which is accompanied by a prayer page for December 13. Because of the preservation of most of the prayer pages, the entire contents of the prayer book can be largely reconstructed. Several Northern saints, such as Louis, King of France, Louis of Toulouse, and Martin of Tours, can be identified. Many of these saints were venerated by the Visconti at Pavia. That noble family's patron saints are also portrayed in the book, but since most affluent Northern Italian families had connections with Northern Europe, this does not identify the book's original owner with any certainty. Such information must have been conveyed by the missing pages, which may have contained portraits or the armorial devices of its proud possessor. Perhaps the lost leaves were removed by descendants, who did not want it known that their heritage had been sold. Michelino's prayer book, at least in its present state, lacks those references to the owner's rank, property, and interests that often personalize devotional works, including Books of Hours.

The prayer book is meant to be seen within the context of the church service, lit by flickering candles and colored, radiant shafts piercing the stained-glass windows. Music was heard and the scent of incense filled the nave as these pale yet strongly colored pages, heavy with embossed gold, were turned. Their delicious, shimmering color seems almost transparent. Light appears to come right through the vellum as if the page itself were translucent. We can imagine that the artist, skilled as he was in the making of stained glass, used his experience in that medium to master illumination. Amazingly, despite the bulkiness and naiveté of some of the figures and the crowded narrative scenes, there is a constant upward movement, a quality of weightlessness, of celestial transcendence in these unprecedented pages.

As Pächt first noticed, three scenes from the Morgan manuscript restate those painted by Michelino in an earlier Book of Hours for the use of Pavia (Avignon, Bibliothèque Municipale, Ms. 111). More delicate than the New York prayer book, the Avignon Hours includes scenes in very pale tints that are suggestions rather than statements. Like polychromed ivories, they have only touches of color, are only hints of illumination. All architectural references are omitted, creating an effect of almost iconic simplicity.

The Avignon *Nativity* is a more immediate presentation of the subject. Mary lies on the ground just after having given birth. The woman washing the baby is shown testing the water's temperature, in much the same pose as the woman in the Morgan manuscript. Nevertheless, the treatment here is more conservative than in the New York *Epiphany (fol. 6v)* and follows traditional Italian formulae. Often dated around 1395, the Avignon manuscript must be separated by at least a decade from the one in New York.

The sole dated examples of Michelino's style after 1414 are the recently restored stained-glass windows for the Chapel of Saints Quirico and Giulitta in the Milan Cathedral, which he completed between 1423 and 1425 (mentioned above). Allowing for radical differences of medium, size, and technique, the windows' apostles display the master's departure from the style of the illuminated pages. There is a new toughness and breadth of treatment here that is far removed from the International Style still so strongly felt in the Morgan Library's book. Not only does the prayer book predate the cathedral windows, but it must also be placed well ahead of the 1414 *Epistles of Saint Jerome*. The latter shows a more fluid, mannered style than the Morgan manuscript, showing a new connection with French art. By the 1420s Michelino was about fifty years old. He may well have abandoned manuscript illumination by that time, saving his creative energies for works of a larger scale, which would be easier on his eyes and more readily and richly rewarded.

If we look at the moving *Entombment (fol. 24v)* and related subjects in the New York manuscript, they show a bold, direct approach entirely consonant with the naive aspects of the courtly vision of the opening years of the fifteenth century. Previous scholars of the prayer book, Schilling and Castelfranchi-Vegas, have been led, therefore, to suggest a date early in the century for the prayer book, and this seems entirely correct.

The year Michelino is known to have been in Venice, 1410, provides a plausible date for the Morgan illumination. If the decorations on the temple floor *(fol. 11v)* are read as the letter "C," it is tempting to interpret this as a reference to Cornaro (Corner) patronage. The same family, as you may recall, commissioned the magnificent Jerome illumination from the Lombard artist in 1414. Lest such prominent reference to a "mortal" patron be seen as implausible as well as improper, remember that the Visconti as well as Maréchal Boucicaut plastered the walls of heaven and earth with references to their crests and other armorial devices.

Renaissance legend has it that as a young boy Giotto was once found in a field, intently drawing a lamb on a large, flat rock. In a similar apocryphal vein, it was said that Michelino was found drawing little animals and small birds while still an infant, blessed with the gift of art before he had the power of speech. The liveliest of the animals in the prayer book is Saint Luke's young ox *(fol. 75v)*, shown cradling the Evangelist's Gospel in his forelegs as he looks up lovingly at his master. Luke's emblem is very much like one frescoed by Michelino on a vault of the church of Sant' Eustorgio, but there the ox is perched catlike on the Gospel and is given halo and wings. In the *Nativity (fol. 2v)*, an older and wiser beast looks down at the naked babe in his manger and warms the infant Jesus with his breath.

Marvelous renderings of a mallard duck and a game bird, very much alive though headed for sacrifice *(fol. 11v)*, are still in the style and spirit of the ornithological studies in the Bergamo notebook of Giovannino de' Grassi. Horses are drawn with a special brilliance. Saint Martin's lively steed *(fol. 80v)* and those of the Magi *(fol. 6v)* recall the equestrian images in Milanese illustrations of the Arthurian cycle popular at the end of the fourteenth century but have a life and force all their own.

Secure in the knowledge that he will prove a far more welcome gift to the Christ child than any old reliquary, a cheetah rides in the retinue of the Magi *(fol. 6v)*; camels, horses, and a falcon follow behind. Such a variety of wild beasts were found in the Christmas play that had been staged in the great piazza before the cathedral of Milan since the mid-fourteenth century. It is possible that many of Michelino's exotic animals were drawn at such a performance. As a Visconti protégé, the artist must have seen their precious zoo in the gardens of the palace at Pavia. He would also have been familiar with the animal studies by Giovannino de' Grassi. The young artist doubtless owned a pattern book comparable to that of Giovannino. Sadly, the master's series of animal studies, bound in a little vellum book treasured by the Vendramin family in the early sixteenth century, is long lost. It was described as a great masterpiece filled with colored zoological renderings. Luckily, the wonderful beasts of the prayer book survive, harbingers of those by Gentile da Fabriano, Jacopo Bellini, and that most popular *animalier* of the fifteenth century, Pisanello.

Each miniature in the Morgan manuscript, along with its facing page, is surrounded by an airborne trellis. Blossoms wind their way around the narrow gold borders, heaven their apparent destination. Golden roots, waving gently in the margin below, appear to have pulled themselves from the sheltering earth, permitting the illuminated page and its prayer to rise. Their presence, as Schilling suggests, may be a decorative extension of the *Carra Herbal*. That these sacred scenes and holy words are already in a state of grace is made explicit by the heavily embossed golden background of many verso pages, on which a hundred flowers echo, in diminutive scale, those found around the borders. Golden stars and dots, sprinkled about the margins, provide additional punctuation.

The stunning contrast between the large flowers growing freely around the borders and the tiny blossoms patterning the golden background provides tension, surprise and movement. Like a good preacher, the artist relies on tempo as well as insight to capture the attention and engage the faith of his audience.

Glowing pools of gold form halos that often go straight down at the sides. The gold then pours in thick, molten rivulets over the back of the page, through row upon row of flowers that seem to reflect the sun or candle flames. As the leaves are turned, these bright bosses shimmer evoking a *locus* and *spiritus* that is quintessentially medieval.

Bold flowers abound in Michelino's manuscript. Their striking presence recalls the phrase so beloved by the Victorians, "The language of the flowers." This metaphor dates back to antiquity, when many plants were treasured for their medicinal and symbolic properties. Christianity simply appropriated this floral vocabulary for the purposes of ecumenical salvation, a word whose meaning is closely related to that of healing. Flowers, so often linked with curative qualities and with divine beauty, were themselves symbols of loving faith and its triumph over death.

Otto Pächt, the scholar who first attributed the Morgan Library's prayer book to Michelino, was also the first to credit the new scrutiny of nature by the Milanese artists of the late Trecento with an influence that led to the naturalism of the early Renaissance. Magnificent herbals and guides to healthy life were illuminated for the Visconti court at Pavia and for their contemporaries the Carrara at Padua, providing a new view of the world as it was—in fact and in faith.

The *Tacuinum Sanitatis,* or *Notebook of Health,* was illustrated with scenes that put words into action. Unlike the herbals, the *Tacuinum* always put information about plants into a human context. This new sense of activity and engagement is felt throughout Michelino's manuscript. Even in those scenes where saints stand alone or in pairs, the power of the flowered background lends stimulus. Faith and healing, the observed and believed, work precariously together, as is illustrated by the manuscript's mirroring of the plants that provide both border and backdrop. The saving presence of flowers is a visual equivalent to the prayers and the images they enclose.

Impatient with the minutiae of clinical botanical detail, Michelino captures the floral image with far less deliberate description than was typical of the masters of the manuscript workshops in which he was trained. His dynamic borders and backdrops achieve a new level of floral fantasy, which was carried on in Northern Europe by the Limbourg brothers in the borders of their *Très Riches Heures*.

Michelino too chose many flowers for their symbolic and medicinal associations. The star-shaped, blue blossoms of borage growing around St. Paul *(fol. 49v)* were believed to be flowers of heaven tied to Christ and the Virgin in their promise of Paradise. Beneficial on earth as well as in heaven, borage, according to the widely read medieval naturalist Albertus Magnus, was good for the blood. It is cited in the *Garden of Health* as a cure for dizziness and palpitation. That most Christian of virtues, humility, was linked to what grew close to the ground, humus. Those fruits, vegetables, and flowers that showed a moral sense of "knowing their place" by shyly hiding their beauty among their own leaves or surrounding grass most particularly exemplified goodness. That is why Michelino chose to depict the violet, pea, and bean blossoms for his floral borders and backgrounds.

Medieval encyclopedists like Pierre Bersuire, whose words were read all over Europe, saw the world as a mirror of salvation and many of its plants as allegories of Christian qualities. Michelino may have selected the beanlike plant, or pea blossom, entwined around the *Entombment (fol. 24v)*, because the Burgundian scholar had written that the bean was the symbol of Christ Incarnate. Bersuire wrote that the bean was able to grow spontaneously, as did Jesus in the womb of the Virgin, and that its nutritious contents revived the earth, corresponding to Christ's deliverance of the world through his Passion.

The heavenly blue cornflowers in the border of the *Resurrection (fol. 26v)* were chosen as the floral equivalent of the earthly symbol of Christian sacrifice—the Eucharist. As the body of Jesus was present in the host, made of wheat, so was His sacrifice manifest by the presence of the heavenly flowers growing in the fields among the sheaves.

Expressive to the point of caricature, Michelino could show the apostles and saints as passionate country bumpkins, rude, possessed, physically ugly in the urgency of their spiritual concerns. Seized by emotion, consumed by caring, these figures are so responsive to vocation as to be oblivious of all but their belief. Such a dramatic, compelling sense of message is felt throughout the narrative scenes in the Morgan book. The artist deliberately confined the Passion Play to a very small area, crowding the characters into a narrow space where confrontation cannot but occur.

In the scene of the *Annunciation (fol. 16v)*, the Angel Gabriel can barely be squeezed into the porch's delicate architectural setting as he kneels before the Virgin of Humility seated patiently on the ground. The great sweet peas of the border wave their blossoms excitedly as though all nature wanted to share this initial moment of redemption. Gabriel's drapery is tinted the same pink as the pea blossoms on the border.

The *Presentation in the Temple (fol. 11v)*, the *Washing of the Feet (fol. 19v)*, the *Finding of the True Cross (fol. 33v)*, and the *Ascension (fol. 35v)* all share this allusion to human bodies caught up by Divine will. Of all the scenes in the narrative cycle, only the *Entombment (fol. 24v)* and the *Resurrection (fol. 26v)* have a greater sense of space. In them Michelino returns to early fourteenth-century formulas that stressed a more static, grander setting and that may have had their roots in Tuscany. This formal amplitude has symbolic resonance— Michelino allows burial space for the dead Christ and living space for His Resurrection.

In some of the narrative scenes two distinct subjects are compressed into very shallow space. As the *Nativity (fol. 2v)* takes place in the foreground, for example, the *Annunciation to the Shepherds* goes on at the upper right. Pairs of angels direct divine light from the Father to the Son, as another angel in the corner announces Christ's birth to the shepherds. While Joseph, Mary, and a holy woman gaze upon the naked, newborn babe, another woman, in the foreground, is preparing a bath. A sense of feverishness is provided by the golden, Van Gogh–like whorls over a blue sky found in the *Annunciation (fol. 16v),* the *Epiphany (fol. 6v),* and the *Finding of the True Cross (fol. 33v).*

The way in which Michelino has grouped the apostles surrounding the Virgin in the *Ascension (fol. 35v)* is unusual. Were it not known that the manuscript also had a depiction of the Pentecost on the lost folio 37 verso, it would seem that this scene was meant to combine both subjects in one. The lost Pentecost would have taken place in an interior to provide contrast with the Ascension, which occurs in a setting similar to the one in which *Christ washes the Feet of the Apostles (fol. 19v).*

Most beautiful of the flowered-background pages with paired figures is the *Visitation (fol. 52v),* which is almost Oriental in the exquisite calligraphic elegance of its presentation. Pressed close to one another, the pregnant Mary and

Elizabeth are almost seen as one. The two women show Michelino's remarkable ability to combine inner and outer grace. His biblical heroines never dwindle away into fashion plates of the International Style.

Forthright in rendering, some of the standing single and paired male saints in the Morgan's manuscript suggest similar statues carved by Northern and Lombard sculptors for Milan's new cathedral. We know that Michelino worked on some of these sculptures. He probably drew the figures in the prayer book using a pattern book of figures equally applicable to sculpture and painting. Considering the strict conventions relating to the depiction of saints, it is likely that some of these holy standing images were left by the artist for execution by his workshop, which is known to have been active as early as 1401. Four very fine colored drawings of standing apostles in the Louvre, by Michelino's hand, suggest the sort of models that could have been followed by his assistants for many commissions in both painting and sculpture.

Strangely, the illumination of a prayer to the Trinity (fol. 39v) makes no visual reference whatever to the triune God. A single figure, the Lord, is shown seated within a mandorla surrounded by fourteen angels. A similar disregard for the conventions of depicting the Trinity is found in Michelino's 1414 Epistle of Saint Jerome. There the mourning God the Father holds the Dead Son. The Holy Ghost, the third member of the Trinity, almost invariably included in this particular grouping, is conspicuously absent.

The Entombment (fol. 24v) is also a conventional subject, but here, as in the Trinity, Michelino's treatment is not. As Longhi noted, the painter broke away from the decorative mold of the International Style as sponsored by the Visconti, returning to the early Sienese manner of Simone Martini, which was more passionate and graceful. The fruit trees Michelino depicts, promises of the Resurrection, suggest the background of Simone's small *Lamentation* panel in Berlin, painted almost a century earlier.

Most original of Michelino's pages is the one showing Saint Luke as a painter *(fol. 75v)*. Luke's Gospel, filled with intimate, direct information about the life of the Virgin and the Infancy of Christ, had long suggested a specially observant, sensitive listener, with a sympathy for detail and the ability to visualize what the Virgin had told him about great events of the past, The Evangelist was also associated with the role of physician, or healer. In Eastern Christianity many icons of the Virgin and Child were thought to come from Luke's hand. This idea of the Evangelist as artist spread to the West, together with the images believed to be painted by him. In Florence, where artists and apothecaries belonged to the same guild, the former purchasing their rare pigments from the latter, the legend of Luke as artist was particularly popular.

In the Introduction to his *Treatise on Painting,* written at the end of the fourteenth century, Cennino Cennini invoked "God the Father, the Son, the Holy Ghost, the Virgin Mary, and St. Luke the Evangelist, the First Christian Painter." By then many artists' guilds were formed in Luke's name, and their chapels often had altarpieces showing the saint in the act of painting the Virgin. The earliest painting recorded of this subject was placed on the altar of the guild chapel in Florence in 1383, where Cennini must have seen it. In his *Lives of the Artists,* Vasari wrote that Agnolo Gaddi, a Florentine painter of the late Trecento, had a "Michele da Milano" as his student. Michelino's page with Saint Luke has a slightly Florentine quality to it and, if we trust Vasari's words, it is possible that Michelino worked in Florence with Gaddi, where he too would have seen the painting in the guild chapel.

If the Morgan manuscript dates from about 1410, it may be the earliest surviving western depiction of Luke as artist. Michelino's page conforms with the proportions of an early altarpiece, very likely vertical in format. Shown painting a half-length Virgin and Child in an engaged frame, Luke is holding a composition closer in style to Northern Italian than to Florentine examples. It may, in fact, be an "updated" version of one of the many paintings of the subject believed to have come from the Evangelist's hand. Though Luke might well be satisfied with his glorious work, he seems reluctant to let the little panel go, cradling it in much the same way that the painted Virgin holds her Son.

When Longhi wrote about the Morgan prayer book, he characterized Michelino as a Watteau of the International Style—an artist with a faint but eloquent reticence, a delicate quality of courtly melancholy. Luke's expression as he paints is one of sad resignation, for he is portraying the Mother and Son he knew and loved. Though the young ox encourages him, Luke seems to know his best is not good enough. Happily the same is not true for Michelino's art. Reflecting, but not restricted by the courtly views of the early fifteenth century, his luminous scenes continue to surprise us, both by sorrow and joy.

Colin Eisler

SELECTED BIBLIOGRAPHY

The Morgan manuscript was first published in a funda-
mental article by Otto Pächt. "Early Italian Nature
Studies and the Early Calendar Landscape." *Journal of the
Warburg and Courtauld Institutes* 13 (1950):13–47.

An excellent study devoted to the prayer book is by Rosy
Schilling. "Ein Gebetbuch des Michelino da Besozzo."
Münchner Jahrbuch der bildenden Kunstj 3rd series, 8 (1957):
65–80.

Another article, concentrating on the connections between
the manuscript and northern art, which follows Pächt's lead
but stresses the importance of the work to the Master of the
Boucicaut Hours, is by Liana Castelfranchi-Vegas. "Il Libro
d'Ore Bodmer di Michelino da Besozzo e i rapporti tra
miniature francese e miniature lombarda agli inizi del Quattrocento." In *Études d'art français offertes à Charles Sterling,*
edited by Albert Châtelet and Nicole Reynaud, pp. 91–103.
Paris; 1975.

For documentation of Michelino's life, see C. Baroni and S.
Samek Ludovici. *La Pittura Lombarda del Quattrocento,* pp.
40–54. Messina-Firenze; 1952.

The great work on early Lombard art remains Pietro
Toesca. *La Pittura e la miniatura nella Lombardia.* Milan; 1912.

The catalogue issued in conjunction with the Milanese
exposition *Arte Lombarda dai Visconti agli Sforza* with an
introduction by Roberto Longhi was printed in Milan, 1958.

Stella Matalon, *Michelino da Besozzo et l'ouvraige de Lombardie,* Milan: Fabbri, 1966, presents an attractive introduction to the subject.

The codicological analysis of the Morgan manuscript was prepared by William Voelkle. The author has benefited from a conversation with Eliot Rowland. An unpublished University of Pennsylvania dissertation by David Sellin, *Michelino da Besozzo,* completed in 1975, has not been consulted by this writer.

PLATES AND LEGENDS

Editor's Note:

Of the forty-seven prayers which are included in the text, only twenty-two of the full page miniatures have survived in the original. Evidence from collation data suggests that the remaining twenty-five prayers must have had full page miniatures as well. Throughout this edition the subjects of the missing miniatures are stated in brackets and their matching surviving prayer page with floral border indicated by folio number. We have endeavored throughout to reproduce the exact page order of the manuscript as it is currently assembled in the Morgan Library.

The Nativity

(NATIVITAS IĤU XP̄I)

December 25

In this miniature Mary kneels with head uncovered and hands joined in prayer before the Infant in the manger. To the left, an aged Joseph leans forward in a gesture of awe. Two midwives attend the Holy Family. One of the women, wearing a pale green gown, crouches in the foreground as she prepares the bath and tests its temperature with her right hand. Swaddling clothes and a silver-bladed knife are set before her and sticks for the fire are placed to her right.

The traditional ox and donkey look benignly at the sacred occupant of their manger. A covering for the child hangs in front of the donkey. Two pairs of angels flank the heavenly rays that hover above the Child. In the distance two shepherds tending their flocks in a barren winter landscape receiving tidings of Christ's birth from an angel. The golden skies imbue this nocturnal scene with brilliance and symbolize the dawn of a new era.

The miniature is bordered with violet flowers resembling pea blossoms, symbol of humility and the Incarnation—Christ made flesh. Golden roots appear at the bottom of most of these pages. *(fols. 2v-3)*

Verbum caro factum est
alleluya. Et habitauit in
nobis alleluya. Oremus.

Regina angelorum do
mina mundi mater
eius qui mundat mu
dum genitrix uite anime me
e. altrix reparatous carnis
mee lactatrix saluatous toti
us substantie mee fígula uni
uersalis pietatis causa gene
ralis reconciliationis uias et
templum uite et salutis uni
uersorum. Tu nanque domi
na admirabilis singulari uir

Circumcision

January 1

The miniature once facing this page, presumably a representation of the Circumcision of Christ, has not been preserved. The prayer appointed for this day begins with the invocation: *"Ihesu nostra redemptio amor et desiderium . . . ."* The first letter, "I," is historiated and depicts a Crucifixion against a solid gold ground. *(fol. 5)*

The Adoration of the Magi

(OBLATIO TRIUM MAGORUM)

January 6

Flanked by the two midwives who may have been depicted in the preceding miniature, Christ receives the homage of the Magi. The Star that has led the kings to Bethlehem shines over the stable as the aged Melchior kneels and kisses the Child's foot. Blessed by Jesus, the king has removed his crown and has handed a golden reliquary to Joseph. Balthazar, traditionally depicted as a beared, middle-aged man, and the youthful Caspar also bear receptacles for the Christ Child. The Magi are accompanied by a colorful retinue that includes a falconer and a lively menagerie of two camels, four horses and a cheetah.

Paired violet blossoms with five petals and gold centers frame this miniature. *(fols. 6v-7v)*

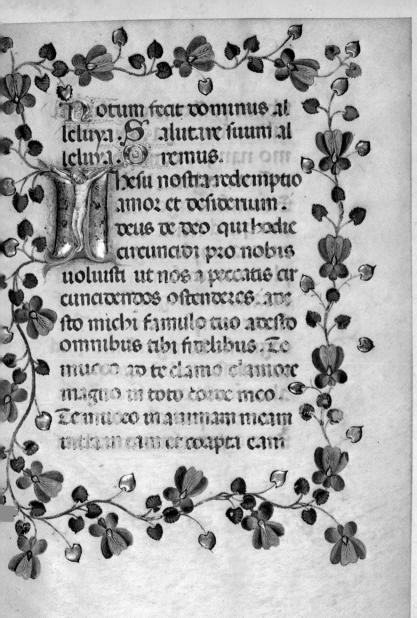

Notum fecit dominus al
leluya. Salutare suum al
leluya. Oremus.

Ihesu nostra redemptio
amor et desiderium.
deus de deo qui hodie
circuncidi pro nobis
uoluisti ut nos a peccatis cir
cuncidendos ostenderes. ade
sto michi famulo tuo adesto
omnibus tibi fidelibus. Te
inuoco ad te clamo clamore
magno in toto corde meo.
Te inuoco in animam meam
intra in eam et corripe eam

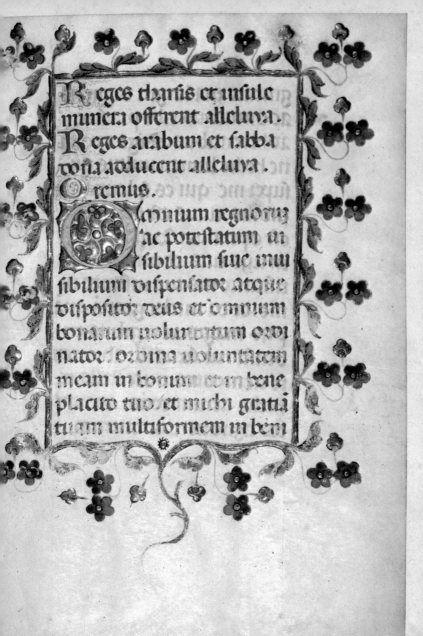

Reges tharsis et insule
munera offerent alleluya.
Reges arabum et sabba
dona adducent alleluya.
Oremus.

Omnium regnorum
ac potestatum in
sibilium siue inui
sibilium dispensator atque
dispositor deus et omnium
bonarum uoluntatum ordi
nator: ordina uoluntatem
meam in bonum: et in bene
placito tuo: et michi gratia
tuam multiformem in beni

gnitate tua largiri digneris
ac omnibus tibi pia fide
adherentibus. Signa domi
ne hodie lumen uultus tui
super me / qui es splendor mi
rabilis cuius est totū quod
est optimum. Viuifica me
in uijs tuis / et uirtutē sanc
tificationis tue infunde in
me. et da michi gratiā quā
pijs magis ac regibus tri
buisti. ut sicut illi ab orien
te uenientes duce stella te
hodie uerum deum adoran
tes agnouerunt / aurum

Saint Anthony

(S̄. ANTONÍ)

January 17

S aint Anthony the Great, revered as the patron of herds-
men, was born in Egypt, near Memphis, about A.D. 250
and is said to have lived to the age of 105. Although he
founded a religious community at Faiyum and established a
monastic rule based on contemplation, his precepts did not
find currency in the West until a much later date. According
to legend, Saint Anthony was tempted by the devil, who
came to him in the desert, offering enticement and delights,
only to be soundly driven back by the abbot's steadfast
refusals. Saint Anthony's life was written by a disciple, Saint
Athanasius. The monk was venerated as a healer who could
cure erysipelas, known as Saint Anthony's Fire. Anthony is
traditionally represented as an aged, bearded abbot; here he
displays a crozier and a book in his left hand, and carries a
silver bell in his right, as in Michelino's Siena panel. The little
black pig usually shown with this saint has been omitted.
Highly stylized blue, five-petal flowers with gilded stamens
and extravagantly voluted leaves frame the miniature. The
blossoms are repeated against the gold background.

(fols. 8v-9)

S. Antoni.

f. 8 v°

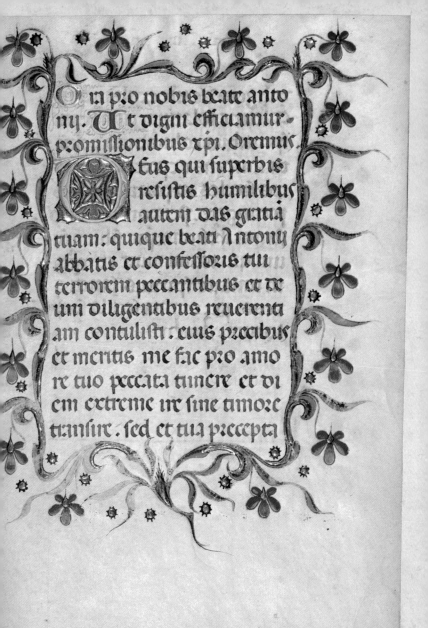

ra pro nobis beate anto
ny. Et digni efficiamur
promissionibus xpi. Oremus.
Deus qui superbis
resistis humilibus
autem das gratiam
tuam: quique beati Antony
abbatis et confessoris tui
terrorem peccantibus et te
um diligentibus reuerenti
am contulisti: eius precibus
et meritis me fac pro amo
re tuo peccata timere et di
em extreme ire sine timore
transire. sed et tua precepta

The Purification of the Virgin

(PURIFICATIO VIRGINIS MARIE)

February 2

The purification of the Virgin is believed to have taken place forty days after the Nativity. Bringing the Child to the Temple in Jerusalem, Mary hands Him to the aged priest Simeon, who stands behind a richly appointed altar.

To the rear of the temple, Joseph displays the two turtle-doves that, according to Luke 2:24, Mary brought as an offering. The Virgin, in a blue robe lined with green, is also attended by two women (perhaps the midwives present at the Nativity and the Adoration of the Magi); one carries a brace of game birds and has a covered basket on her shoulder. The older woman, behind Simeon, dressed in black and wearing a halo, is probably the prophetess Anna, who is mentioned in Luke 2:36–38. The dark green floor bears a pattern resembling that depicted in the miniature on folio 73v. The scene is framed with gold-centered blue flowers. Each flower has four blue petals and is shown from the top and in profile.

(fols. 11v-12v)

[Border page: *St. Agnes*, January 21. *fol. 10*]

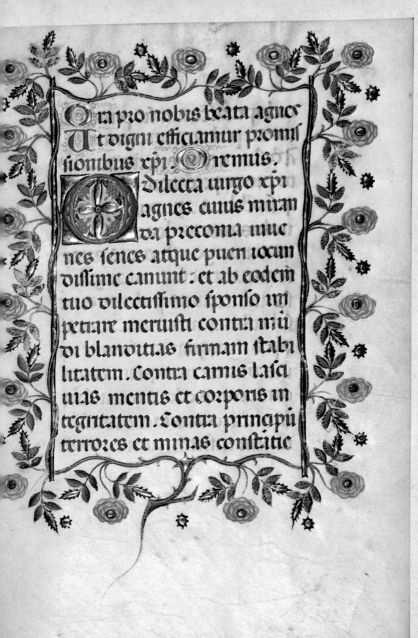

Ora pro nobis beata agnes
Ut digni efficiamur promis
sionibus xpi. Oremus.

Dilecta virgo xpi
agnes cuius miran
da preconia iuue
nes senes atque pueri iocun
dissime canunt: et ab eodem
tuo dilectissimo sponso im
petrare meruisti contra mu
di blanditias firmam stabi
litatem. Contra carnis lasci
uias mentis et corporis in
tegritatem. Contra principu
terrores et minas constitie

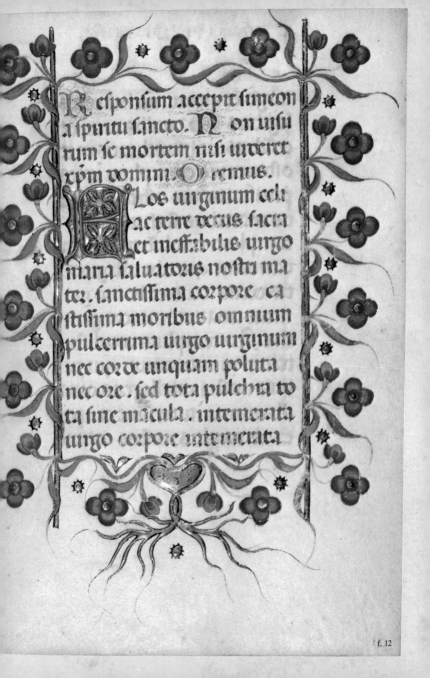

Responsum accepit simeon
a spiritu sancto. Non uisu
rum se mortem nisi uideret
cpm domini. Oremus.

Flos uirginum celi
ac terre decus sacra
et ineffabilis uirgo
maria saluatoris nostri ma
ter. sanctissima corpore ca
stissima moribus omnium
pulcerrima uirgo uirginum
nec corde unquam poluta
nec ore. sed tota pulchra to
ta sine macula. intemerata
uirgo corpore intemerata

uirgo et mente. nichil debes
legibus / quia nullis tacta ex
cessibus. ut humilitatis in te
ostenderes exemplum iples
purificationis officium. polu
tis matribus statutum. Ad
templum detulisti tecū mun
dandum / qui tibi integrita
tis decus / deus et homo ge
nitus adauxit intacta geni
trix. Ad templum detulisti
tecum mundandum qui de
licta nostra intelligens quia
illi omnia nuda sunt et aper
ta ab occultis nostris cotidie

Saint Blaise

(SCS BLASIUS)

February 3

Saint Blaise was the bishop of Sebastea in Armenia; he was tortured and then beheaded near the city walls around A.D. 316, for refusing to make offerings to pagan gods. Here Blaise is dressed as a bishop. He wears a bejeweled mitre with pearls, a gold-bordered cape, a surplice, white gloves, and two rings on his left hand. He holds a crozier in his left hand; in his right, he displays a currier's comb, the instrument of his martyrdom.

The narrow landscape rises to form two grassy hillocks. Violets, symbolizing humility, drawn in profile, surround the miniature. The same motif, vertically linked by slender green tendrils, appears against the background. *(fols. 14v-15v)*

Ora pro nobis beate blasii
Ut digni efficiamur promis
sionibus xpi. Oremus.

Advocat te anima mea
qui fecisti me ut non
obliuiscaris oblitum
tui. et exquirentem te nec de
seras uita que nunquam mo
reris. Deus une deus trini
tas in cuius ualde misericor
dia confido salus esto infir
mitati mee et uerus resusci
tator anime mee. Et quia pec
cator ac indignus te rogare
presumo meritis saltem pi

issimi martiris tui atque pō
tificis blasij cuius hodie sol
lempnia recenseo me exau
dire digneris. ac doce me
patientiam ad sustinendū
aduersa. doce me scientiā
scripturarum ut sic loquar
ne superbiam sic taceam
ne torpescam sic contine
ut non cadam sic stringe ut
non dimittas. Tu es enim
honor meus et laus mea
et fiducia mea ac omnium
xpianorum xpe saluator.
Qui uiuis et regnas deus

The Annunciation

March 25

The scene of the Annunciation takes place within an elaborate architectural setting, reminiscent of a Gothic church though closed off by a green curtain with a round-arched portico. The Virgin is seated on the floor, in an attitude of humility. Her blue dress matches her mantle, which is lined in green. The Old Testament, probably turned to Isaiah 7:14, which says, "Behold, a Virgin shall be with child and bring forth a son," lies open on her lap. Mary's head is uncovered and her right hand is raised in surprise at the arrival of Gabriel, whose wings are red and blue with gold highlights. The Archangel, on one knee, hails Mary: *"Ave Maria, gratia plena. . . ."*

Three golden rays, issuing from the bust of God the Father in the upper left-hand corner, stream toward the Virgin's head as the Holy Spirit, symbolized by a little dove, descends on one of them toward her head. The dove flies toward Mary's ear, illustrating the concept of the "word made flesh," because according to medieval theology, conception took place through her ear. The delicacy of this composition is enhanced by the use of tender pinks and greens, keyed to the border of pea blossoms, symbols of humility.

(fols. 16v-17v)

f. 16 v°

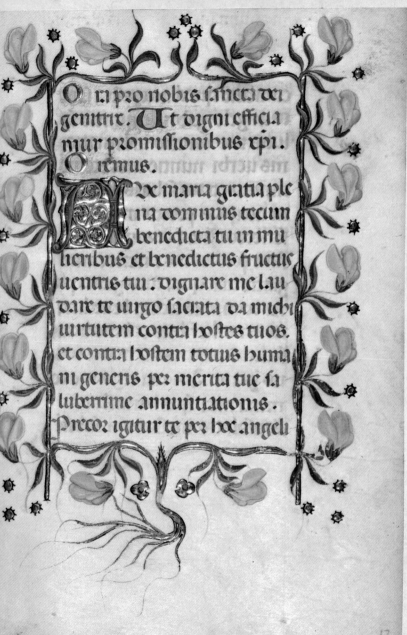

Ora pro nobis sancta dei
genitrix. Ut digni efficia
mur promissionibus xpi.
Oremus.

Aue maria gratia ple
na dominus tecum
benedicta tu in mu
lieribus et benedictus fructus
uentris tui. dignare me lau
dare te uirgo sacrata. da michi
uirtutem contra hostes tuos.
et contra hostem totius huma
ni generis. per merita tue sa
luberrime annuntiationis.
Precor igitur te per hoc angeli

f. 17

cum aue quod accepisti a sancto angelo gabriele nuntio salutis tue nuntio incarnationis uerbi nuntio uite eterne nuntio etiam salutis nostre. ut accipias preces meas misericordissima domina. magna sunt peccata mea maior autem gratia tua. quia tu es gratia plena dominus tecum benedicta tu in mulieribus et benedictus fructus uentris tui mater totius gratie. Domina ergo mea domina mea spes humilium. consolatio mestorum subste

Christ Washing the Feet of the Apostles

(IN DIE IOVIS SANCTA)

Thursday of Holy Week

In this crowded scene, which precedes the missing sequence of miniatures illustrating the events of Easter Week, Christ is shown on His knees, washing the feet of Saint Peter. It seems that two other apostles are removing their shoes to have their feet washed. The significance of Christ's act of humility is poignantly reflected in Peter's gesture of despair and by the somber expressions of the eleven apostles in the background. John the Evangelist is the young figure at the far left. This scene is a fine example of Michelino's gift for characterization.

Although the architectural setting is unexceptional, the painter achieves unusual pictorial effects through the contrast of warm and cool tones and the translucency of the pigments. At the top, blue sky is visible. A wreath of stylized lavender-colored larkspur forms the border to this miniature.

(fols. 19v-20v)

[Border page: *Christ Bearing the Cross*, Good Friday (?). *fol. 21*]

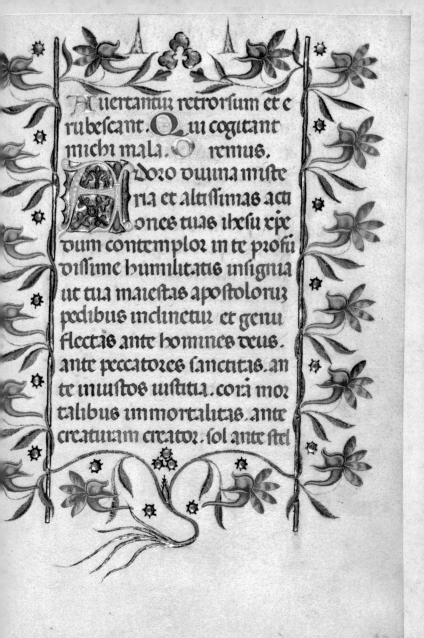

Auertantur retrorsum et e
rubescant. Qui cogitant
michi mala. Oremus.

Adoro diuina miste
ria et altissimas acti
ones tuas ihesu xpe
dum contemplor in te profu
dissime humilitatis insignia
ut tua maiestas apostolorum
pedibus inclinetur et genu
flectas ante homines deus.
ante peccatores sanctitas. an
te iniustos iustitia. cora mor
talibus immortalitas. ante
creaturam creator. sol ante stel

las. lux ante tenebras. et laudes
inclinatus omnium rex regu
et dominus dominantium ut
nullius creature tanta possit es
se humilitas quin tua non sit
ipsa profundior. Dum etiam
contemplor te agnum dei paci
ficum sacerdotem summum et
pontificem verum hodie tradi
disse discipulis tuis carne tu
am immaculatam hostiam pu
ram hostiam vivam. et sangui
nem tuum in ultima et nobili
cena ad manducandum et bi
bendum. Per huiusmodi exi

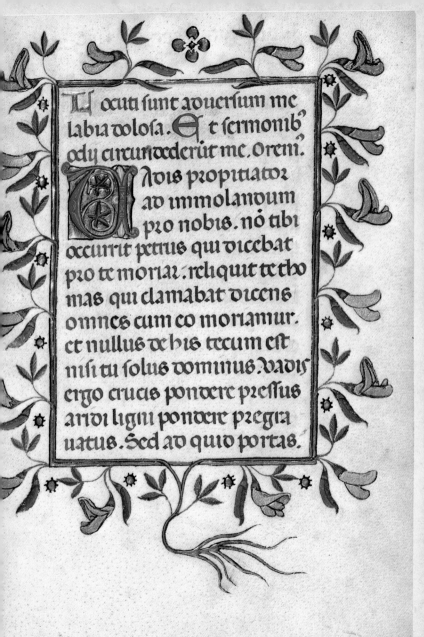

Locuti sunt aduersum me
labia dolosa. Et sermonib9
odij circundederunt me. Oremus.
Dois propitiator
ad immolandum
pro nobis. no tibi
occurrit petrus qui dicebat
pro te moriar. reliquit te tho
mas qui clamabat dicens
omnes cum eo moriamur.
et nullus de his tecum est
nisi tu solus dominus. vadis
ergo crucis pondere pressus
aridi ligni pondere pregra
uatus. Sed ad quid portas.

The Entombment

(SABBATO SANCTO)

Saturday of Easter Week

In this scene of concentrated grief, the artist combines highly charged, emotional expression with an exquisite sense of decoration. Joseph of Arimathaea and Nicodemus are shown carefully placing Christ's body into a pink marble tomb; through the arched entrance a lamp and a sarcophagus are partially visible. The Virgin, Saint John the Evangelist, and the three Marys look on in attitudes of anguish. Mary Magdalen kneels with her hands clenched in sorrow. The dramatic impact of the composition is vividly sustained. The emphasis on Christ's stocky martyred figure in the foreground is intensified by the concerted attention of the mourners massed by the tomb.

The feeling of sorrow that pervades this representation of the Entombment is in marked contrast with the depiction of nature, which is seen as bountiful and verdant. According to John 19:41, the sepulchre was erected in a garden. Some of the details in this scene may symbolize life, death, and the Resurrection of Christ. The pea blossom, symbol of humility, and pods compose the border. *(fols. 24v-25v)*

[Border page: *Crucifixation*, Good Friday (?). *fol. 22*]

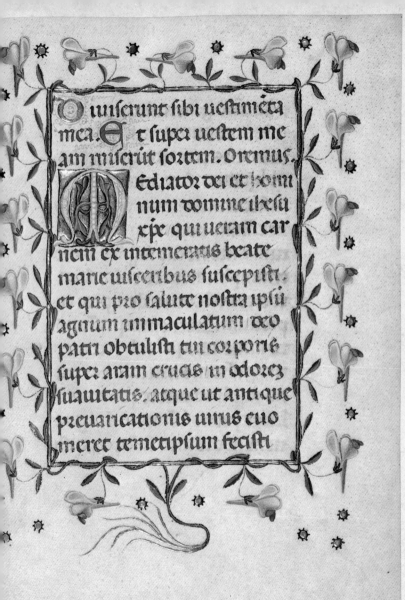

iuserunt sibi uestiméta
mea. Et super uestem me
am miserút sortem. Oremus.

Ediator dei et homi
num domine ihesu
xpe qui ueram car
nem ex intemeratis beate
marie uisceribus suscepisti:
et qui pro salute nostra ipsū
agnum immaculatum deo
patri obtulisti: tui corporis
super aram crucis in odorē
suauitatis. atque ut antique
preuaricationis uirus euo
meret temetipsum fecisti

Caro mea requiescet in spe.
Et non dabis sanctum tu
um uidere corruptionem.
Oremus.

Domine ihesu xpe q
i uoco in sepulcro re
quiescere passus es
ut nos de sepulcris nostris ei
ceres et tue resurrectionis glo
ria sanares adesto supplicatio
nibus meis et presta ut post
finem huius labilis uite sit
michi in sepulcro meo te iu
bente quieta dormitio et in
die iudicy cum omnibus sac

tis leta resurrectio . Tu me do
mine tibi totum uendica to
tum posside nullamq; in me
partem a te uacare permitte
sed solus in me uiuas et me
tibi soli uiuere facias . Qui
uiuis et gloriaris uerus deus
per omnia secula seculorum
Amen.

The Resurrection

(RESURRECTIO IHU XPI GLIOIA)

Easter Sunday

This splendid composition depicts the resurrected Christ standing on the marble tomb illustrated in the preceding miniature. The large boulder sealing the entrance has not yet been rolled aside; it is still firmly attached with metal strips and emphasizes the miraculous nature of the event. Christ raises His right hand in blessing; in His left He displays a banner signifying His victory over death. The Lord's wounds are made visible through an opening in His drapery. We notice, in particular, the wound on His right made by a soldier's lance after the Crucifixion. We can see, too, the dots of blood marking the crown of thorns placed on Christ's head when he went before Pilate and later removed.

Three soldiers, posted to guard the sepulchre, slumber in the foreground; others lie sleeping behind the tomb, which is hedged with spears propped against its roof. There is a Resurrection in the *Epistles of St. Jerome* that has a similarly colored tomb with the stone still in front, sealed with the same metal strips. The use of metallic pigment to represent the color of the armor is exceptional here. Its use is repeated in folio 33v, *The Finding of the True Cross*.

The luminous tones of Christ's robes and of the tomb are offset by the brilliant blue of the cornflowers in the border and background. Growing among the corn, these flowers were believed to be close to Christ and so able to save one from death. *(fols. 26v-27)*

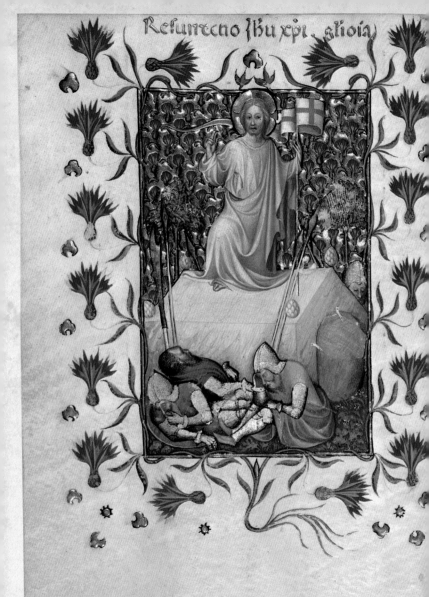

Surrexit dominus de sepulcro. Qui pro nobis pependit in ligno alleluya. Oremus.

Summa sapientia simplex deitas lux inaccessibilis perfecta bonitas desiderata clementia agnus dei uerbum patris uita salus redemptio spes nostra domine ihesu xpe mortis destructor et uenie largitor humiliter oro ut me digneris trahere post te ut ueniam ad te quem adoro natum pacem tenens portantem que adoro

Saint Philip and Saint James Minor

(S̄ PHILIPPUS. S̄ JACOBUS)

May 1

T he apostles Philip and James Minor (or the Less) are both venerated as martyrs of the early church. Saint Philip was stoned to death at Hierapolis in Phrygia. In this miniature he is portrayed as an elderly apostle with a long beard, wearing a blue robe and pink mantle. In his right hand he displays a tall cross; in his left, a book bound in green.

Saint James, the son of Alphaeus and Mary Cleophas (one of the three Marys), was Christ's cousin. He became the first Bishop of Jerusalem, where he was put to death for preaching the Gospel. He is shown in a white robe and blue mantle, carrying a pink book bag. Both saints stand barefoot in a narrow, leafy landscape. The miniature is bordered with small mauve blossoms, which are repeated against the gold background. *(fols. 30v-31v)*

[Border page: *St. George of Cappadocia*, April 23. *fol. 29*]

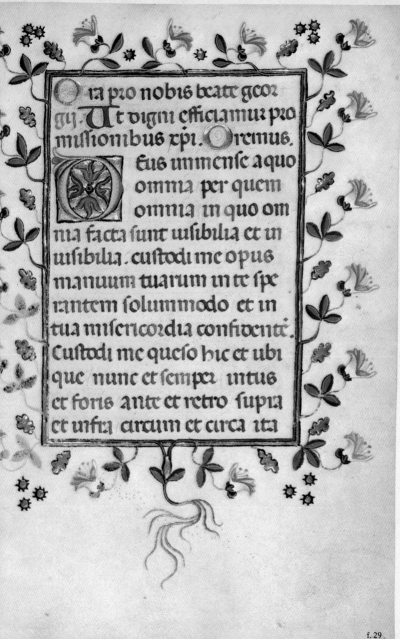

ora pro nobis beate geor
gij. Ut digni efficiamur pro
missionibus xpi. Oremus.
Deus immense a quo
omnia per quem
omnia in quo om
nia facta sunt visibilia et in
visibilia. custodi me opus
manuum tuarum in te spe
rantem solummodo et in
tua misericordia confidentē.
custodi me queso hic et ubi
que nunc et semper intus
et foris ante et retro supra
et infra circum et circa ita

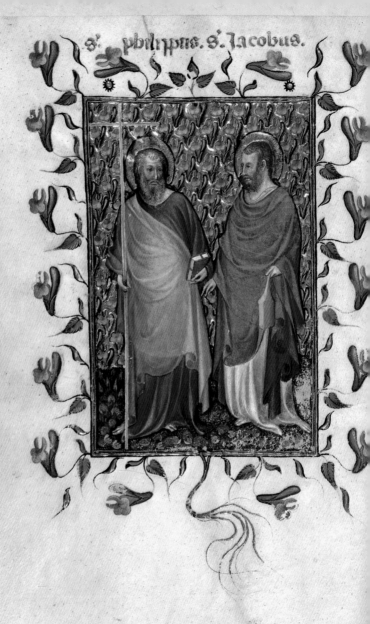

f. 30 v°

Nimis honorati sunt amici
tui deus. Nimis conforta
tus est principatus eorum.
Oremus.

Innumeris miraculis
ac meritis fulgentes
amici dei philippe ac
iacobe, quorum anime in ce
lo triumphant, corpora in ter
ris requiescunt, adeste nunc
uocati pariter precibus meis
moti. Vos celi ianitores atqʒ
seculi senatores et iudices cū
magistro uestro futuri domi
ni nostri ihesu xpi. Ego de gre

ge xpi ouis licet minima ue
stre tamen cure deputata et
doctrinis uestris initiata sub
uestrum presidium confugio
que per multas illecebras ab
errando diu deuia fere perij.
Ego scilicet immanis peccator
omnibus flagitijs et facino
ribus obnoxius deprecans
obnixius ut ad exemplũ ma
gistri uestri pastoris optimi
qui posuit animam suam pro
ouibus suis me lupinis mor
sibus sublatum et contagio
uitiorum uestris meritis et

The Finding of the True Cross

(INVENTIO SANCTE CRUCIS)

May 3

Empress Helena, the wife of Constantine Chlorus, was the mother of Constantine the Great. Helena is also believed to have found the true cross, which, according to Gregory of Tours, occurred on May 3, A.D. 326. (This accounts for the tie between the event and May 3.) She brought a part of the cross back to Rome.

At least four separate events said to have occurred over many days are represented here. Helena is shown with her retinue of female attendants and courtiers in fur-lined hats and eight soldiers, prominently displaying both her power and rank, as she interrogates Judas. She points to the fire she used as a threat if Judas wasn't found and to the dry well in which he was confined for seven days to coerce him to reveal the site of the cross. In the foreground, to the right, two diggers uncover the three crosses; Christ's bears the *titulus,* placed nearest to the viewer.

The visual impact of the scene is further enhanced by the use of brilliant, metallic accents to represent armor; these make an effective contrast to the somber browns, blues, and grays dominating the color scheme. The framing motif is a pinkish pea-blossom type, keyed to the tones of Judas's cloak.

(fols. 33v-34v)

f. 33 v°

Hoc signum cruas erit in ce
lo alleluya. Cum dominus
ad iudicandum uenerit allelu
ya. Oremus.

Aue crux gloriosissima
omnium lignorum
pretiosissima et splen
dissima que tactu conditoris
es sanctificata et eius glorio
sissimo sanguine cruentati. fe
lix permanens et permanebis
in secula. pretiosissima cunctis
arboribus extitisti nó decore
frondium propriorum aut
pulchritudine florum siue di

gnitate fructuum sed castissi
mis membris regis eterni quod
sustinuisti unde omne redi
meres seculum. Ipse enim est
fructus tuus suauissimus de
cor tuus splendidissimus odor
tuus flagrantissimus. dulce
lignum dulce pomum dulces
palmas dulce onus sustulisti
tu sola felix talentum mundi
portasti. Tibi ergo domine
ihesu xpe qui in huiusmodi li
gno pependisti humiles pre
ces offero pro me et pijs om
nibus et oris uota persoluo

The Ascension

(ASCENSIO IHU XPI)

Forty days after Easter

In this dramatic illustration of Christ's Ascension, the Virgin, sometimes included in such scenes, is portrayed in an attitude of humility, her hands crossed high on her breast. She is shown surrounded by eleven apostles, all kneeling as they gaze heavenward in awe. In the stance and deeply serious expressions of these stocky, heavily draped figures, Michelino aptly conveys the feelings of the apostles as they watched Christ ascend to Paradise. Jesus is shown with arms outstretched, as if in flight, in a flowing, pale blue robe; he wears a cruciform halo. He is accompanied by three pink-winged trumpeting angels. Two angels, perhaps the "men in white" mentioned in Acts 1:9, address the assembly below. Leafy green branches are seen against the dark blue background.

Christ's Ascension is accentuated by the diagonal flutter of his drapery and the angle of the trumpets and golden rays, all leading to the upper right. Even the pale bluish flowers run on the same diagonal. *(fols. 35v-36)*

Ascendit deus in iubilatice
alleluya. Et dominus in uo
ce tube alleluya. Oremus.

Supplicatio mea ascé
dat ad te xpe intret
in conspectu tuo ora
tio mea deus, perueniat depre
catio mea ad te domine. qui
triumphator hodie super om
nes celos ascendisti. Qui de
uicto mortis imperio, huma
nitatis spolia unde ueneras
reportasti. oro te ihesu xpe ne
nos deseras orphanos, fran
gat te pietas uiscerum tuorú

Holy Trinity

(SANCTA TRINITAS UNUS DS)

First Sunday after Pentecost

This magnificent and richly hued composition is an emblematic representation of the Holy Trinity. Without any visual reference to a tripartite deity, God is shown seated on a rainbow within a mandorla supported by fourteen red angels. His right hand is raised in benediction as He holds an orb with a cross above. Golden rays emanate from the seated figure.

This is an unusually delicate rendering, with more technical refinement in evidence than in most of the others. Layer upon layer of color create a sense of depth like that of stained glass or transparent oil glazes. Periwinkle blossoms (Vinca Major) twine about the border. This flower's star shape and blue color may be symbolic of heaven, the flower of Christ, the Virgin Mary, and the Angels. *(fols. 39v-40v)*

[Border page: *Pentecost*, Fifty Days after Easter. *fol. 37*]

[Border page: *Corpus Christi*, Thursday after Trinity Sunday. *fols. 42-42v*]

[Border page: *St. Anthony of Padua*, May 10. *fol. 44*]

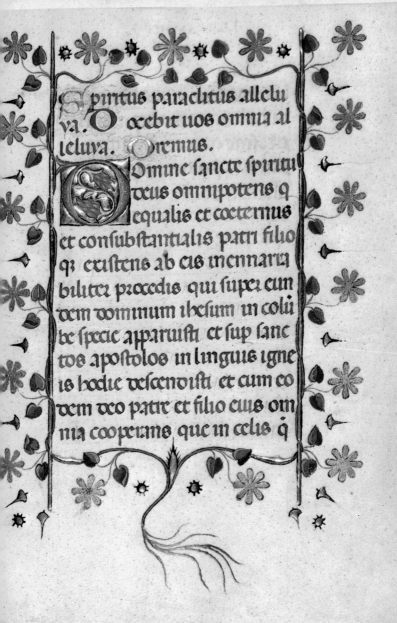

Spiritus paraclitus allelu
ya. Docebit uos omnia al
leluya. Oremus.

Omine sancte spiritu
deus omnipotens q
equalis et coeternus
et consubstantialis patri filio
q; existens ab eis inennaria
biliter procedis qui super eun
dem dominum ihesum in colu
be specie apparuisti et sup sanc
tos apostolos in linguis igne
is hodie descendisti et cum eo
dem deo patre et filio eius om
nia cooperaris que in celis q̃

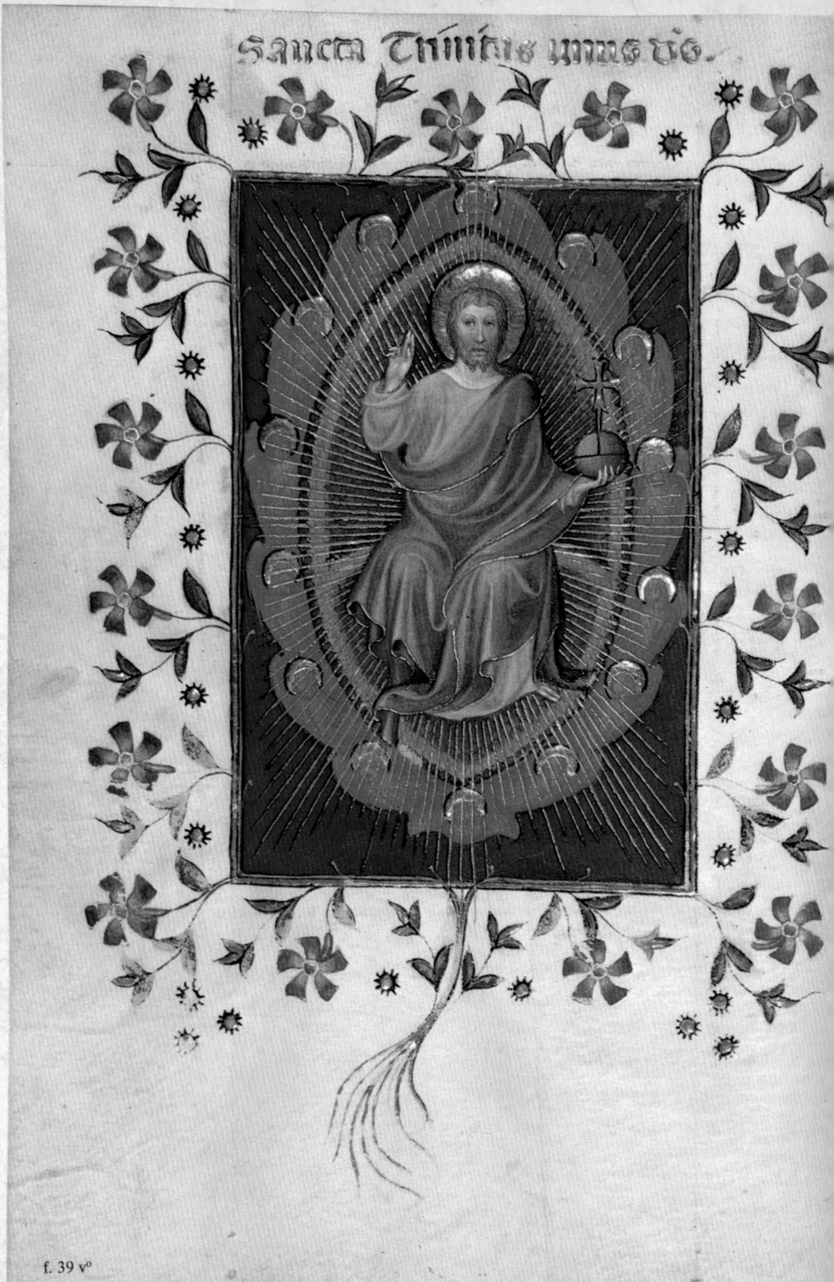

f. 39 v°

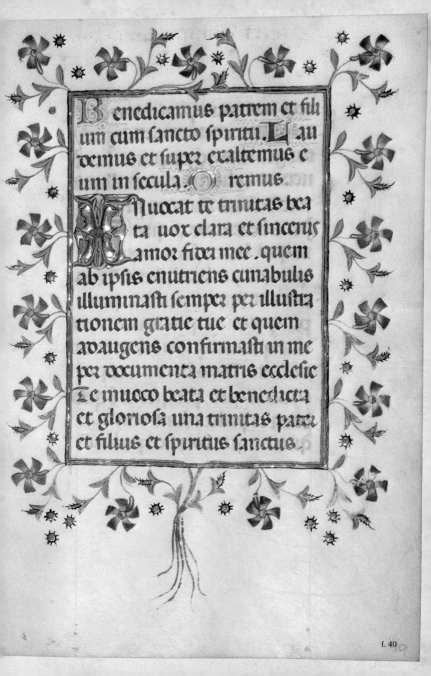

Benedicamus patrem et fili
um cum sancto spiritu. Lau
demus et super exaltemus e
um in secula. Oremus.

Jnuocat te trinitas bea
ta uox clara et sincerus
amor fidei mee. quem
ab ipsis enutriens cunabulis
illuminasti semper per illustra
tionem gratie tue. et quem
adaugens confirmasti in me
per documenta matris ecclesie
Te inuoco beata et benedicta
et gloriosa una trinitas pater
et filius et spiritus sanctus.

deus dominus paraclitus cari
tas gratia comunicatio geni
tor genitus regenerans. lumé
uerum ex lumine uera illumi
natio fons flumen irrigatio.
Deus beatitudo a quo p qué
in quo beata sunt omnia .
queecunque beata sunt. Deus
uera et summa uita a quo
per quem in quo uiuunt om
nia queecunque uere et beate
uiuunt. Deus bonum et pul
crum a quo per quem i quo
bona et pulcra sunt omnia
queecunque bona et pulcra

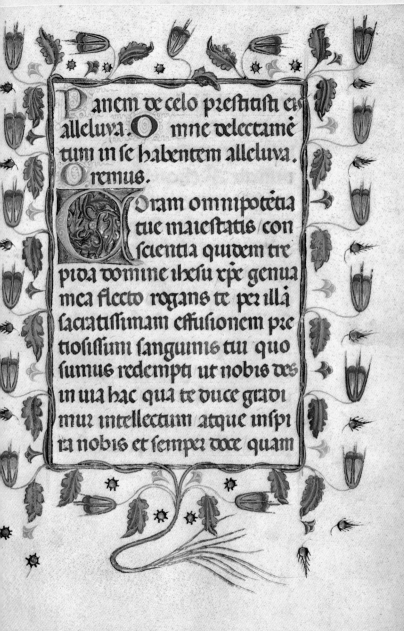

Panem de celo prestitisti eis
alleluya. Omne delectame
tum in se habentem alleluya.
Oremus.

Coram omnipotétia
tue maiestatis / con
scientia quidem tre
pida domine ihesu xpe genua
mea flecto rogans te / per illá
sacratissimam effusionem pre
tiosissim sanguinis tui quo
sumus redempti ut nobis des
in uia hac qua te duce gradi
mur intellectum atque inspi
ra nobis et semper doce quam

inreprehensibiliter sit creden
dum istud misterium ineffa
bile et preceteris intellectu
difficile. Reliqua uero sacra
menta que tenentur in eccle
sia tua domine stupenda sut
et miranda. sed istud tuum
sacramentum quod hodie re
colimus precellit uniuersa.
Nullum enim est isto salubri
us quo purgantur peccata
uirtutes augentur et mens
omnium spiritualium caris
matum abundantia impin
guatur. Hoc nempe celestis

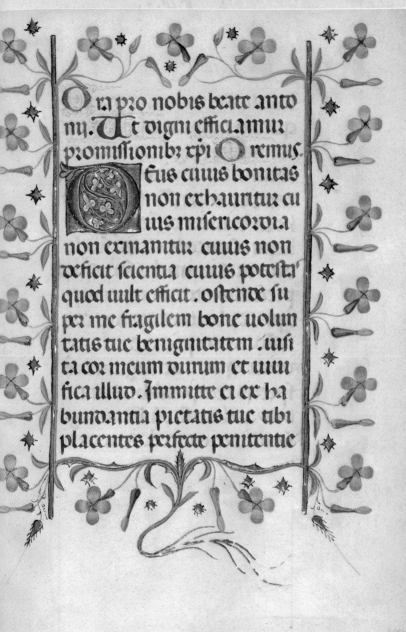

Ora pro nobis beate anto
ny. Ut digni efficiamur
promissionibus xpi Oremus.
Deus cuius bonitas
non exhauritur cu
ius misericordia
non exinanitur. cuius non
deficit scientia. cuius potesta'
quod uult efficit. ostende su
per me fragilem bone uolun
tatis tue benignitatem. uisi
ta cor meum durum et uiui
fica illud. Jmmitte ei ex ha
bundantia pietatis tue tibi
placentes perfecte penitentie

Saint Peter

(SANCTUS PETRUS)

June 29

Saint Peter, called the Prince of the Apostles, became the first bishop of Rome, where, according to legend he was crucified head downward, around A.D. 67. He is generally represented as an elderly apostle, with a broad face and short white hair and beard. Saint Peter is often shown holding a book and the keys to the gates of Paradise, as he is represented here. The landscape in this scene is limited to a narrow grassy plot bordered with small boulders. These perhaps refer to the saint's Latin name, signifying "rock," the foundation upon which Christ's church was built.

Golden pea blossoms and buds form a sumptuous frame to the miniature. These stylized flowers, linked by a wavy, light leaf pattern, are repeated in gold against a strong green background. *(fols. 46v-47v)*

[Border page: *St. John the Baptist*, June 24. *fol. 45*]

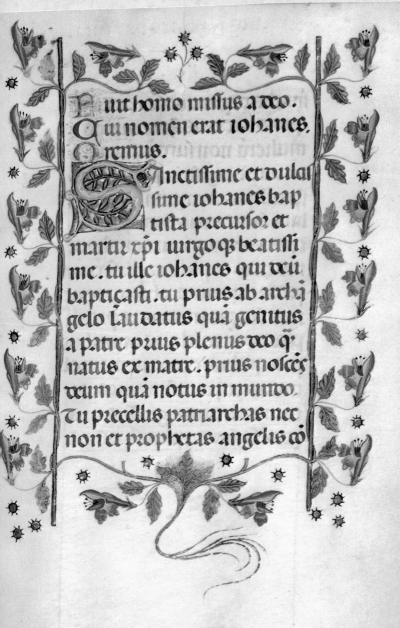

Fuit homo missus a deo:
Qui nomen erat iohanes.
Oremus.

Sanctissime et dulcis
sime iohanes bap
tista precursor et
martir xpi virgo q̄ beatissi
me. tu ille iohanes qui deū
baptizasti. tu prius ab archā
gelo laudatus quā genitus
a patre prius plenus deo q̄
natus ex matre. prius nosces
deum quā notus in mundo.
Tu precellis patriarchas nec
non et prophetas angelis cō

.Sanctus. petrus.

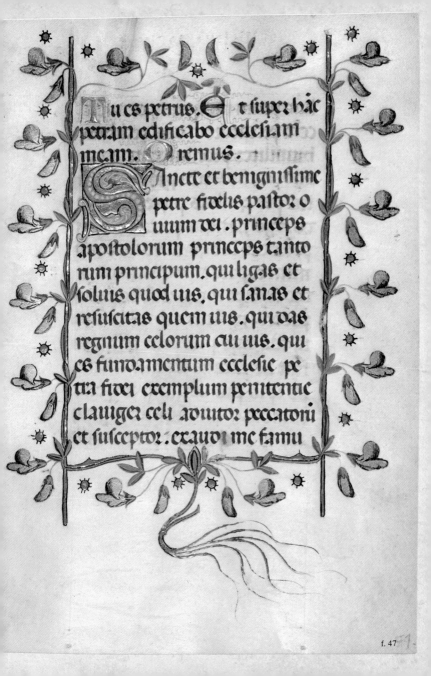

Tu es petrus. Et super hāc
petram edificabo ecclesiam
meam. Oremus.

Sancte et benignissime
petre fidelis pastor o
uium dei. princeps
apostolorum princeps tanto
rum principum. qui ligas et
soluis quod uis. qui sanas et
resuscitas quem uis. qui das
regnum celorum cui uis. qui
es fundamentum ecclesie pe
tra fidei exemplum penitentie
clauiger celi adiutor peccatori
et susceptor. exaudi me famu

lum tuum indignum et infeli
cem peccatorem tuis pedibus
humiliter procumbentem ex
audi omnes tibi pios et fide
les pro quibus preces tibi fun
do. Ego nanque peccator meis
pollutus labijs, tantum domi
num deprecari non audeo. i
deo suscipe meas infelicitatis
preces. ut sicut tabita discipu
la tua tuis precibus restituta
fuit ad uitam, ita tuis meritis
ab ipso pio domino impetra
re merear uiuificantem grati
am spiritum compunctionis

Saint Paul

(SANCTUS PAULUS)

June 30

Saint Paul, a fanatic persecutor of Christians before his conversion on the road to Damascus, is venerated as both teacher and missionary to the Gentiles. According to tradition, he was martyred in Rome in A.D. 67, with his fellow apostle, Saint Peter. Paul is generally portrayed as a balding, bearded, middle-aged man. Here he is shown holding an open book in one hand, a reference to his Epistles, and a great sword in the other. He was martyred by beheading. Paul stands in a grassy landscape, with a small tree and rock formations in the background.

The miniature is framed with blue blossoms of borage and small pinkish buds. The brilliant blue floral motif, combined with a vertical, linking-leaf pattern, is repeated against the gold background, emphasizing the use of blues and greens throughout the composition. Borage, a flower of heaven, was also believed to be good for the blood and for other medicinal purposes. *(fols. 49v-50v)*

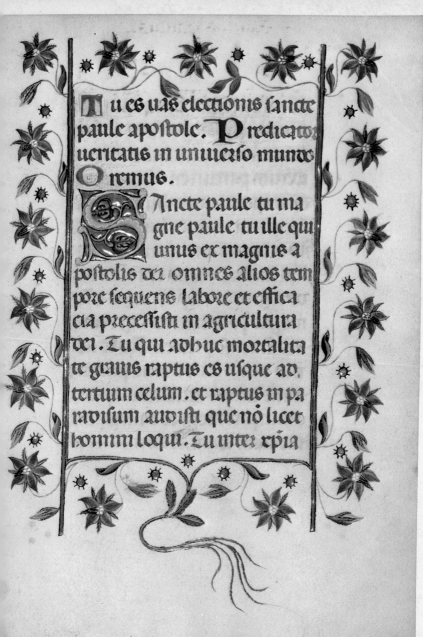

Tu es uas electionis sancte
paule apostole. Predicator
ueritatis in uniuerso mundo
Oremus.

Sancte paule tu ma
gne paule tu ille qui
unus ex magnis a
postolis dei omnes alios tem
pore sequens labore et effica
cia precessisti in agricultura
dei. Tu qui adhuc mortalita
te grauis raptus es usque ad
tertium celum. et raptus in pa
radisum audisti que non licet
homini loqui. Tu inter xpia

nos non solum tanquam nu
trix fouens filios suos sed et
solicitudine mirabilis affectus
iterum parturiens filios tuos.
Tu inquam omnibus omnia
factus ut omnes lucrifaceres
Ao te beatissime ao te his et a
lijs multis dictis et factis mū
do cognitum apud deum esse
magne potestatis et erga homi
nes imense pietatis. Ao te ue
nio unus certe nimis peccator
unus nimis accusatus apud
omnipotentem et districtum
iudicem deum. Non uno non

The Visitation

(SALUTATIO VIRGINIS ET ELISABETH)

July 2

After the Annunciation, Mary traveled to Judah, where her cousin Elizabeth was soon to give birth to Saint John the Baptist. As the women embrace, Elizabeth's welcoming gesture fully conveys her understanding of Mary's visit, as expressed in Luke 12:42: "Blessed art thou among ·women, and blessed is the fruit of thy womb. . . ." The Virgin is clothed in a deep blue robe, lined in green, the colors of faith and hope. Elizabeth, portrayed as an older woman, wears a salmon pink robe and a mauve cloak; her head and shoulders are covered with a white shawl. The scene is framed with delicately shaded violet flowers, which also appear against the gold background. According to Honorius of Autun, violets are found in heaven as they are symbols of humility, one of Mary's most important virtues. *(fols. 52v-53)*

f. 52 v°

Ora pro nobis sancta dei
genitrix. Ut digni efficiamur
promissionibus xpi. Oremus.
Deprecor te domina
sanctissima virgo
maria mater dei per
devotissimam visitationem ac
salutationem quam hodie he
lisabeth fecisti. tu que es pie
tate plenissima summi regis
filia mater orphanorum con
solatio desolatorum via erran
tium salus in te sperantium.
virgo ante partum virgo in
partu virgo post partu. fons

Saint James the Apostle

(SANCTUS JACOBUS APOSTOLUS)

July 25

Saint James Major (or the Greater), son of Zebedee and Mary Salome, was the brother of Saint John the Evangelist and cousin to Jesus Christ. He was beheaded at Eastertide, around A.D. 42, by Herod Agrippa I. The apostle's remains were transported to Santiago de Compostela in Spain, James's principal shrine and a hugely popular center of pilgrimage in the Middle Ages. During the fourteenth century it became customary to represent the saint himself with a pilgrim's hat and a long wooden staff, as he is shown here. In this miniature he carries a green-bound book in his right hand; a pilgrim's hat hangs from a cord about his shoulders. John's robes are arranged to show his bare feet on the barren, rocky landscape, which is studded with cockle shells, his traditional symbol. The shells may be actually lying in the bed of a dried-up stream.

The framing motif is composed of deep blue delphinium blossoms, which are repeated against the gold background. Their golden roots are seen below. The delphinium was believed to cure eye troubles. *(fols. 56v-57)*

[Border page: *Mary Magdalen*, July 22. *fol. 54*]

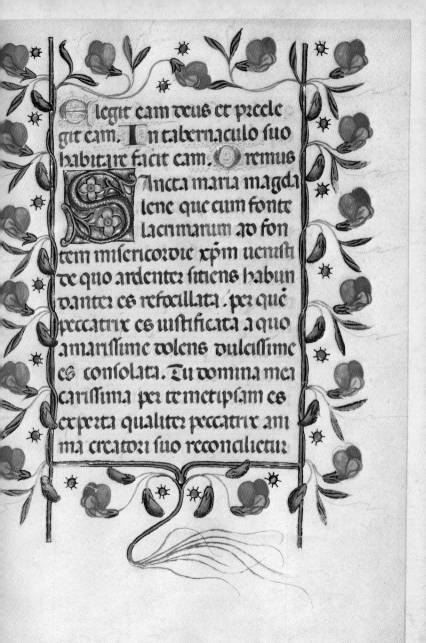

Elegit eam deus et preele
git eam. In tabernaculo suo
habitare facit eam. Oremus
Sancta maria magda
lene que cum fonte
lacrimarum ad fon
tem misericordie xpm uenisti
de quo ardenter sitiens habun
danter es refocillata. per quem
peccatrix es iustificata. a quo
amarissime dolens dulcissime
es consolata. Tu domina mea
carissima per te metipsam es
experta qualiter peccatrix ani
ma creatori suo reconcilietur

Sanctus Jacobus apostolus.

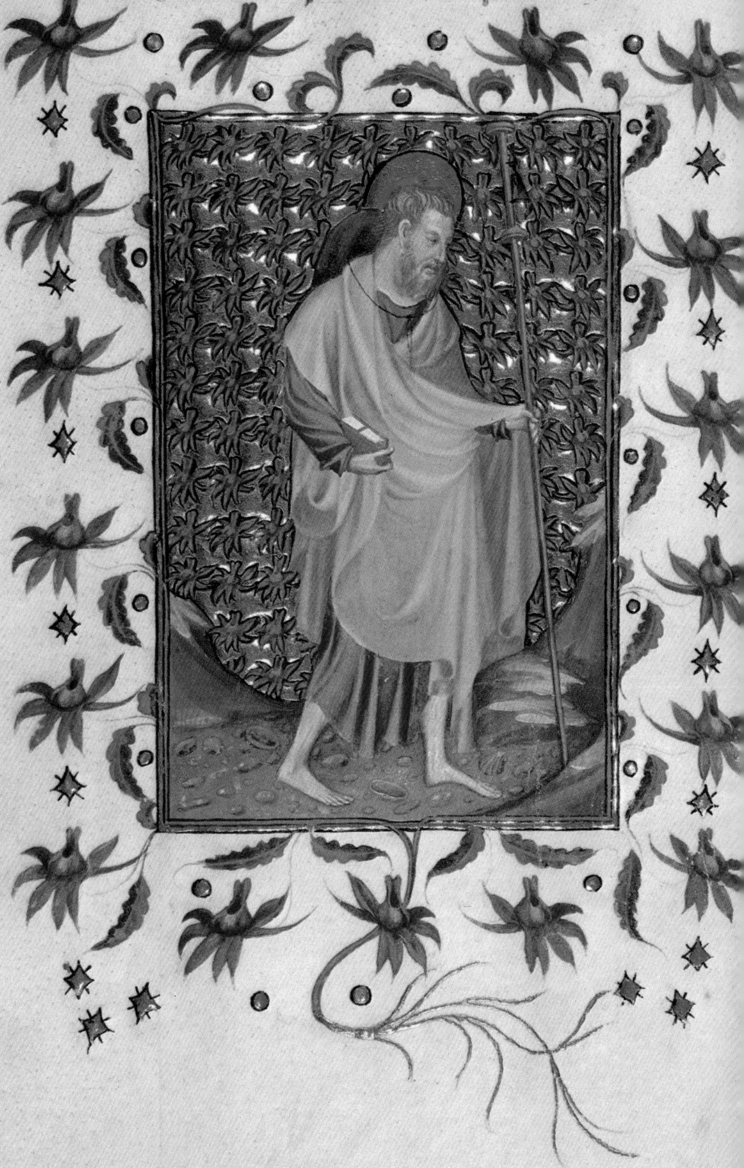

f. 56 v°

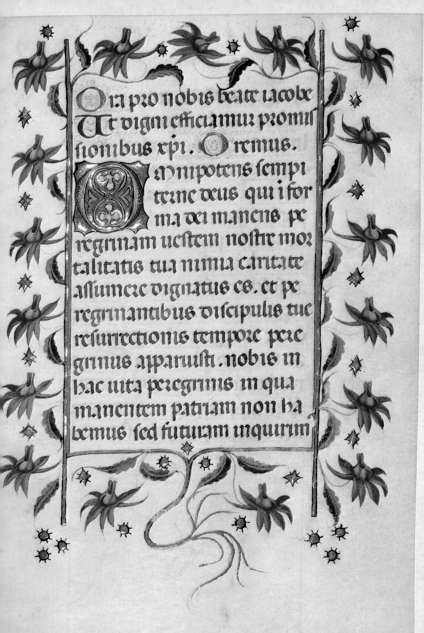

Ora pro nobis beate iacobe
Ut digni efficiamur promis
sionibus xpi. Oremus.

Omnipotens sempi
terne deus qui i for
ma dei manens pe
regrinam uestem nostre mor
talitatis tua nimia caritate
assumere dignatus es. et pe
regrinantibus discipulis tue
resurrectionis tempore pere
grinus apparuisti. nobis in
hac uita peregrinis in qua
manentem patriam non ha
bemus sed futuram inquirim

The following border pages and the continuation of their respective prayers without their facing miniatures correspond to the list of Feast Days below:

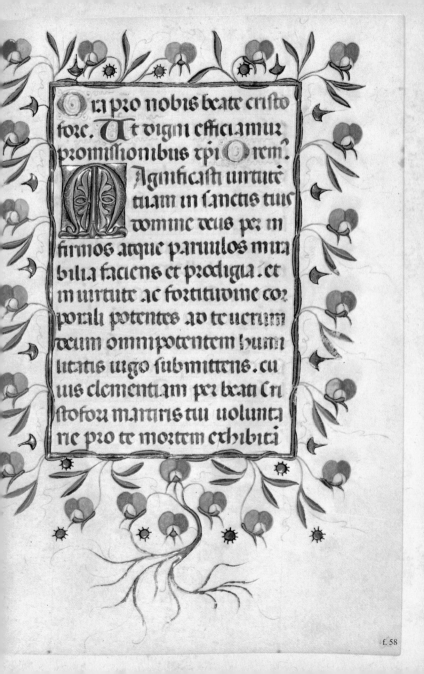

Ora pro nobis beate cristo
fore. Ut digni efficiamur
promissionibus xpi Orem.

Magnificasti virtute
tuam in sanctis tuis
domine deus per in
firmos atque paruulos mira
bilia faciens et prodigia. et
in virtute ac fortitudine cor
porali potentes ad te verum
deum omnipotentem humi
litatis iugo submittens. cu
ius clementiam per beati cri
stofori martiris tui volunta
rie pro te mortem exhibiti

subeuntis tota deuotione de
posco. ut sicut ipsum spreta ui
ta temporali tui solius dedisti
fortissimum zelatorem sic me
sic fideles omnes facias ad per
hennem uitam consequendam
contra mundi temporalia for
tissimos bellatores. per domi
num nostrum ihesum xpm
filium tuum qui tecum uiuit
et regnat in unitate spiritus
sancti deus. per omnia secu
la seculorum. Amen.

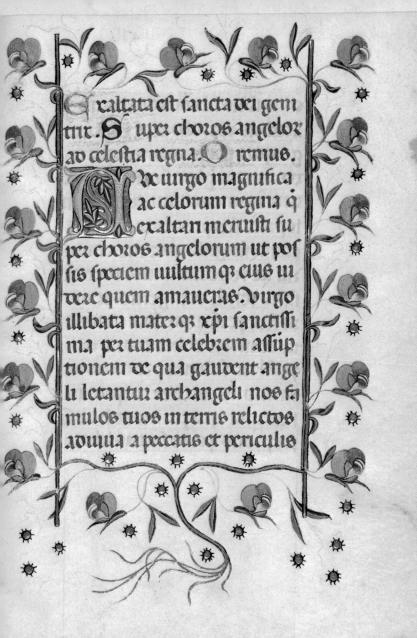

Exaltata est sancta dei geni
trix. Super choros angelor
ad celestia regna. Oremus.

Te uirgo magnifica
ac celorum regina q
exaltari meruisti su
per choros angelorum ut pos
sis speciem uultum q eius in
dere quem amaueras. Virgo
illibata mater q xpi sanctissi
ma per tuam celebrem assup
tionem de qua gaudent ange
li letantur archangeli nos fa
mulos tuos in terris relictos
adiuua a peccatis et periculis

f. 59

omnibus libera ac in bonis
actibus corrobora. Exaudi er
go quia potes omnes qui te
dominam glorificant et sanc
tum nomen tuum cum humi
li prece frequentant. Adiuua
etiam singulariter me domi
na ut residuum uite mee cū
sano sensu et ingenio et ue
ra fide perficiam. Hoc etiam o
ra domina et hoc exora ut
posthac sub tua protectione
mundus corde et corpore in
hac uita qui per me adhuc sū
trepidus per te factus liber

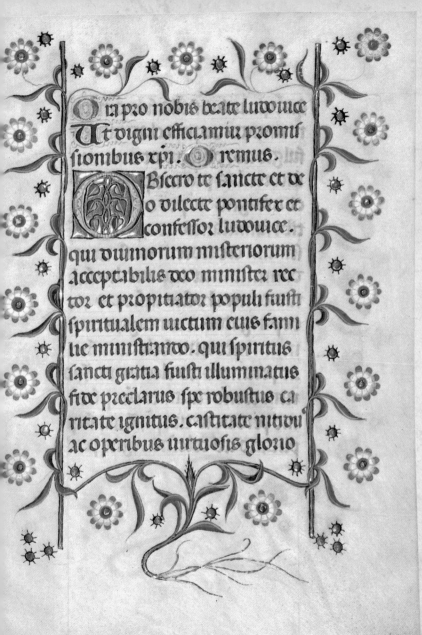

Ora pro nobis beate ludouice
Ut digni efficiamur promis
sionibus xpi. Oremus.

Bscero te sancte et de
o dilecte pontifer et
confessor ludouice.
qui diuinorum misteriorum
acceptabilis deo minister rec
tor et propiciator populi fuisti
spiritualem uictum cius fami
lie ministrando. qui spiritus
sancti gratia fuisti illuminatus
fide preclarus spe robustus ca
ritate ignitus. castitate nitidus
ac operibus uirtuosis glorio

sus. qui uelut stella firmameti
in mundo diuina claritate es
fulgidus. obsecro ut dixi ut
intercedas pro me peccatore
et indigno ac pro omnibus
tibi famulantibus apud altis
simum creatorem nostru et
dominum ut tuo auxilio ful
tus contra hostis insidias et
expurgatus a contagiis om
nium meorum scelerum faci
at pertinere ad electorum suo
rum consortium et cu ipsis
me perducat tua pijssima sup
plicatio ad celestis regni per

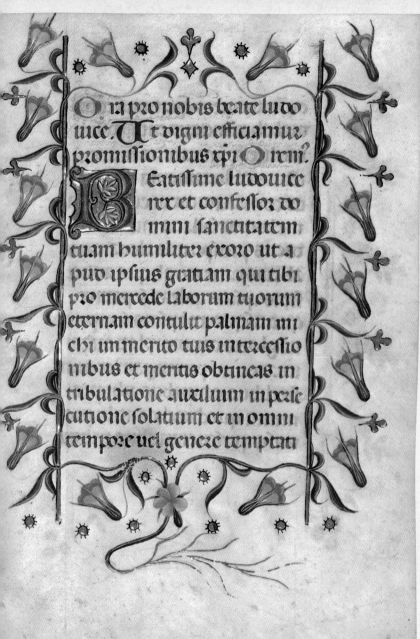

Ora pro nobis beate ludo
uice. Ut digni efficiamur
promissionibus xpi. Orem.

Eatissime ludouice
rex et confessor do
mini sanctitatem
tuam humiliter exoro ut a
puo ipsius gratiam qui tibi
pro mercede laborum tuorum
eternam contulit palmam mi
chi in merito tuis intercessio
nibus et meritis obtineas in
tribulatione auxilium in perse
cutione solatium et in omni
tempore uel genere temptati

omis uirtutem quatinus cōtra
diabolica incitamenta possim
uiriliter dimicare. et mundi
istius oblectamenta superare
ut contra amorem eius nulla
me huius fallacis mundi blā
diens prosperitas eleuare nec
ab eius caritate aliqua aduer
sitas ipsius ualeat separare.
quo usque ad ipsius sempiter
ne glorie contemplationem
una tecum pertingam et cum
fidelibus omnibus ubi pre
mium quod inchoantibꝫ pro
misit perseuerantibus tribuit

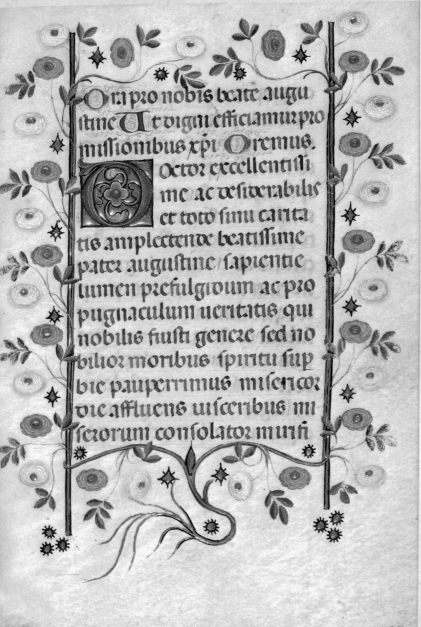

Ora pro nobis beate augu
stine Ut digni efficiamur pro
missionibus xpi Oremus.

Doctor excellentissi
me ac desiderabilis
et toto sinu carita
tis amplectende beatissime
pater augustine sapientie
lumen presulgidum ac pro
pugnaculum ueritatis qui
nobilis fuisti genere sed no
bilior moribus spiritu sup
bie pauperrimus misericor
die affluens uisceribus mi
seroum consolator multi

cus / xp̄m crucifixum seques
nudus / mundo crucifixus.
qui a summo sacerdote xp̄o
es sacerdos preelectus. te q̄
ipsum illi hostiam uiuam in
censanter offerens / in ipso fō
te pietatis tuis affluenter la
crimis ab omni rubigine ui
tiorum immaculatus. prop
ter que nunc sanctorum pre
sulum es stola indutus / coro
nam martirum multiplici la
bore consecutus. apostoloru
collegio meritis et gratia co
equatus. archangelorum be

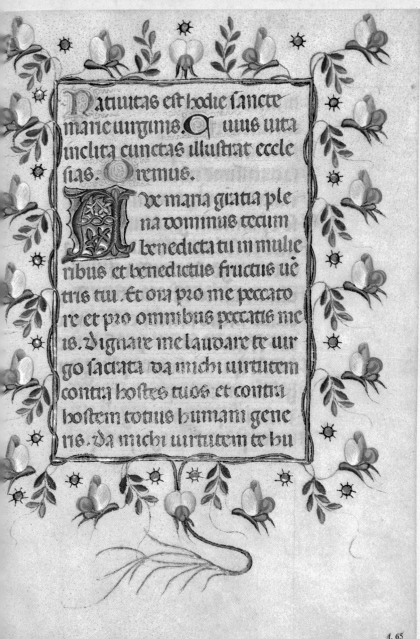

Natiuitas est hodie sancte
marie uirginis. Cuius uita
inclita cunctas illustrat eccle
sias. Oremus.

Ave maria gratia ple
na dominus tecum
benedicta tu in mulie
ribus et benedictus fructus ue
tris tui. Et ora pro me peccato
re et pro omnibus peccatis me
is. Dignare me laudare te uir
go sacrata da michi uirtutem
contra hostes tuos et contra
hostem totius humani gene
ris. Da michi uirtutem te bu

militer deprecandi da michi
uirtutem te cum precibus ob
nixe laudandi. per merita tue
sacratissime natiuitatis qua
natus es in mundum uniuer
se xpianitati gaudium spes
uite et solatium. Quando na
ta es uirgo sacratissima tunc
illuminatus est mundus stirps
beata radix sancta et benedic
tus fructus tuus que sola me
ruisti spiritu sancto plena uir
go deum concipere uirgo do
minum portare uirgo domi
num parere uirgo post par

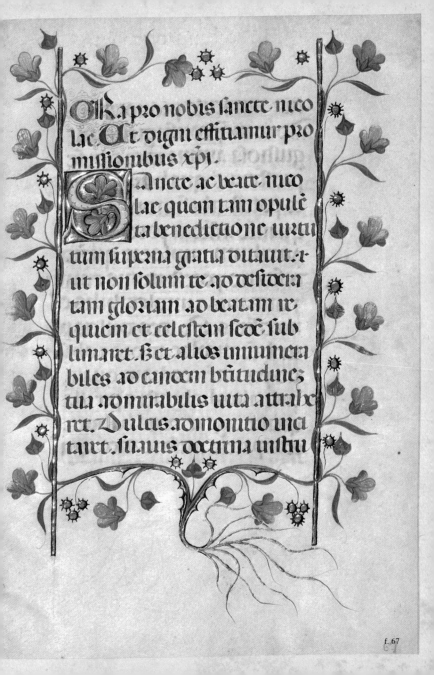

Ra pro nobis sancte nico
lae. Et digni efficiamur pro
missionibus xpi.

Ancte ac beate nico
lae quem tam opule
ta benedictione uirtu
tum superna gratia ditauit. et
ut non solum te ad desidera
tam gloriam ad beatam re
quiem et celestem sedem sub
limaret. sed et alios innumera
biles ad eandem beatitudinem
tua admirabilis uita attrahe
ret. Dulcis admonitio inci
taret. suauis doctrina instru

ciet miracula prouocarent.
Ad te itaq; confugiens an
gustiosa anima mea tibi se
prostrauit qua humili me
te potest tibi fundit preces.
quanto affectu potest tuuz
auxilium implorat quато
desiderio potest nimis enim
7 inmanis 7 intolerabilis e
necessitas. Et ideo dulcis pa
ter bte nicolae te oro 7 obse
cro per misericordiam quam
circa alios habuisti 7 per illa
quam circa te deus habuit.
compatere miserie mee qui

Hoc signum crucis erit in ce
lo. Cum dominus ad iudica
dum uenerit. Oremus.

Alue crux dei uene
randa que sapiētia
lumen et doctrix es
orbis terrarum / que et uera
laus et amica uirtutum et cla
ra phylosophya apud celico
las terrigenas q̄ indesinenter
uiges. quam magis decet im
perialem uocari thronū quā
seruile tormentum. quia im
perator et rex noster xp̄s re
gnum sibi in te et potestate;

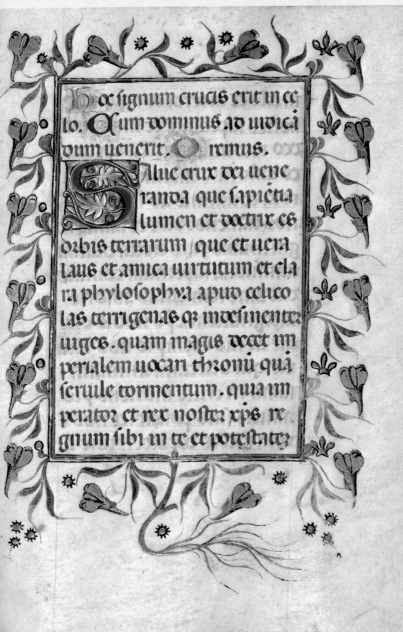

Saint Gall

(SCS GALUS ABBAS)

October 16

Saint Gall, a venerated figure in early church history, left Ireland with Saint Columban around A.D. 585 to revitalize monastic rule on the Continent. On the shores of Lake Constance in Switzerland, he built a cell, which in the eighth century gave rise to the great abbey named after him.

Here Saint Gall is portrayed as a bishop, rather than as an abbot, the way he is customarily shown. The crozier he carries also signifies episcopal status. Wearing a pale blue cape lined with green over his habit, a bejeweled mitre, and fine, gauzelike gloves, he turns his head to the left. The figure stands on a narrow, patterned green ground. Delicately shaded pink flowers, with six petals and light centers, frame the image; the same motif is repeated in regular, closely set rows against the gold background. *(fols. 73v-74v)*

[Border page: *St. Francis of Assisi*, September 17 (?). *fol. 72*]

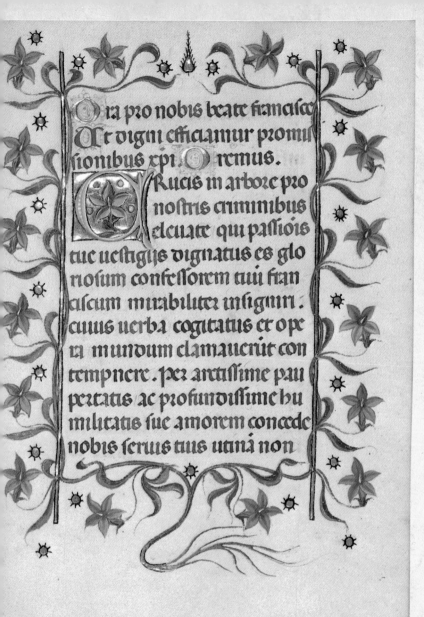

Ora pro nobis beate francisco
Ut digni efficiamur promissionibus xpi. Oremus.

CRucis in arbore pro
nostris criminibus
eleuate qui passiois
tue uestigiis dignatus es glo-
riosum confessorem tuü fran-
ciscum mirabiliter insigniri.
cuius uerba cogitatus et ope-
ra mundum clamauerüt con-
tempnere . per arctissime pau-
pertatis ac profundissime humilitatis sue amorem concede
nobis seruis tuis utiná non

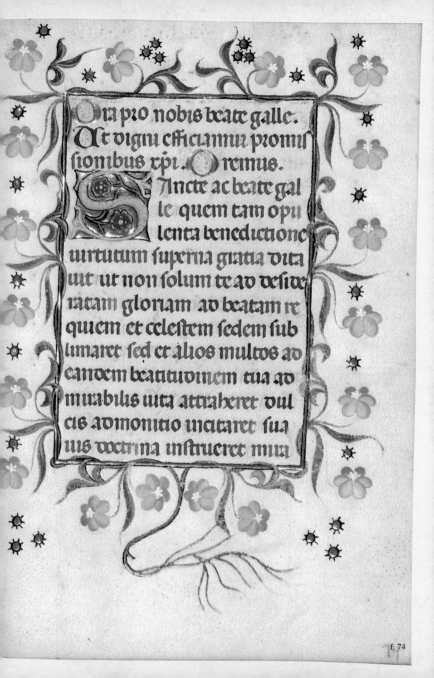

Ora pro nobis beate galle.
Ut digni efficiamur promis
sionibus xpi. Oremus.
Sancte ac beate gal
le quem tam opu
lenta benedictione
uirtutum superna gratia dita
uit ut non solum te ad deside
ratam gloriam ad beatam re
quiem et celestem sedem sub
limaret sed et alios multos ad
eandem beatitudinem tua ad
mirabilis uita attraheret dul
cis admonitio incitaret sua
uis doctrina instrueret mira

cula prouocarent . Ad te confu
giens anima mea tibi se prostra
uit qua humili mente potest
tibi fundit preces quanto af
fectu potest tuum auxilium im
plorat quanto desiderio potest
nimis enim est immanis eius
necessitas . O dulcis pater beate
galle oro obsecro per misericor
diam quam erga alios habui
sti et per illam quam erga te
deus habuit compatere neces
sitati mee ac necessitati omni
um fidelium qui congratula
mur felicitati tue . Succurre te

Saint Luke

(SCS LUCAS EVĀGELISTA)

October 18

Saint Luke the Evangelist, patron of both painters and physicians, is shown here as a massive, sculptural figure. He holds a brush in his right hand as he adds the finishing golden touch to the engaged frame of a painting of the Virgin and Child, held in his left. The artist created the illusion of an interior in perspective, with a knotty wooden floor, low chest at the right, and a lectern at the left. Closed books rest upon the lectern and the chest. The artist-evangelist's small paint pots are scattered on the chest. In the foreground a haloed young ox—the Evangelist's symbol—proudly cradles his master's richly bound Gospel between his forelegs, grazing Luke's green robe. Of all the pages with single figures this is the most delicately balanced. Blue and green, buff, pink and gold are played against one another with the most extraordinary delicacy and subtle resonance. For all the pale pastel coloring, the shimmering blossom-strewn background, there is a sustained note of gravity and solemn insight.

This miniature is an outstanding example of Michelino's subtle use of color. The brilliance of the gold is echoed by the luminous blond tones of the wood, while the delicately shaded blue-green of the saint's robes harmonize with the dusty pink of the blossoms in the border and background. Thought to be a form of nightshade, the flower in the borders was believed to ward off the evil eye and ease heartache.

(fols. 75v-76)

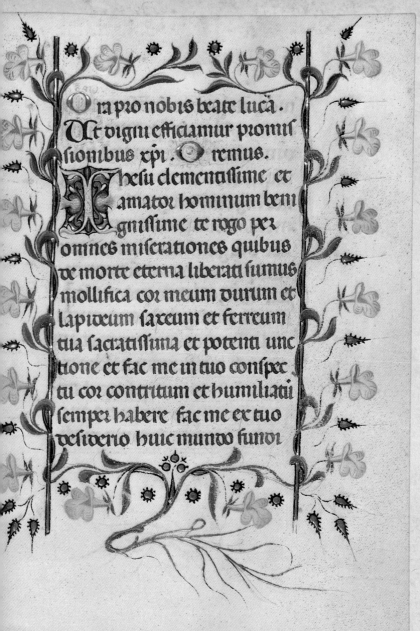

Ora pro nobis beate luca.
Ut digni efficiamur promis
sionibus xpi. Oremus.
Thesu clementissime et
amator hominum beni
gnissime te rogo per
omnes miserationes quibus
de morte eterna liberati sumus
mollifica cor meum durum et
lapideum saxeum et ferreum
tua sacratissima et potenti unc
tione et fac me in tuo conspec
tu cor contritum et humiliati
semper habere fac me ex tuo
desiderio huic mundo fundi

Saint Martin

(SCS MARTIN)

November 11

The Saint (A.D. 316–397) was born in Hungary of pagan parents. Baptized at eighteen, he was befriended by Saint Hilary of Poitiers. Consecrated bishop of Tours in A.D. 371, Martin was widely venerated for his charity to Christian and non-Christian alike. In this forceful miniature, the artist has chosen to illustrate the most celebrated episode in the saint's life, rather than simply portraying him as an isolated figure. Fair haired and bearded, Martin is shown as a Roman officer on horseback cutting his cloak with a short sword to share it with a barefoot, scantily clad beggar standing by the wayside. Later Christ appeared to Martin in a vision, clad in the cape the saint had shared with the beggar. In the background a second rider, with a starlike mark on his hat, may be pointing behind himself. His horse looks away. The use of diagonal elements, the interaction of human and animal figures, and the illusion of depth through landscape distinguish the composition of this remarkably powerful scene. The horseshoe on the raised hoof is a nice detail, and the fine rendering of the horses supports Michelino's reputation as an *animalier*. The image is bordered by pink flowers with five-pointed petals; these are repeated against the gold background.

(fols. 80v-81)

[Border page: *All Saints*, November 1. *fol. 78*]

Exultabunt sancti in gloria
Et letabuntur in cubilibus
suis. Oremus.

Elices sancti omnes
dei qui iam pertran
sistis huius morta
litatis pellagus et peruenire
meruistis ad portum perpetue
quietis securitatis et pacis. Se
curi et tranquilli semp que fe
stiui atque gaudentes estis. ob
secro per matris caritatem uoce
qui secum estis de nobis solici
ti estote de nobis. securi estis
de uestra immarcessibili gloria

Ora pro nobis beate martine
Ut digni efficiamur promis
sionibus xpi. Oremus.
Sancte ac beatissime
martine per illum
te precor qui per to
tum mundum ueneran facit
nomen tuum ne neneges in
digenti et supplicanti auxiliu
tuum. Cui es domine per or
bem ab omnibus uocatus ni
si ut omnium rogantium sis
aduocatus. Aduitor meus sac
te martine ut quid est ubiq;
nomen tuum diffusum nisi

Saint Catherine

(SC̄A KATERINA VIRGO)

November 25

Saint Catherine of Alexandria was the daughter of Sabinella, queen of Egypt, and Costis, the half-brother of Constantine the Great. She was put to death in A.D. 307 at the Emperor Maxentius's orders. The virgin martyr is generally represented as a young princess, sumptuously robed. Here she wears blue and green, the colors worn by the Virgin in this manuscript. Two delightfully rendered angels in blue hover about Catherine's head, one tendering the palm of martyrdom, the other, a crown of martyrdom set with four jewels. Renowned for her great learning, Catherine is shown carrying a blue book bag in her left hand, which rests upon a spiked wheel, symbol of her torture. She was martyred by being beheaded.

The miniature is framed by a variety of pink pea blossoms, a symbol of humility. The plant appears both in bud and full bloom and is shown also in a more stylized form against the gold background. Golden roots are seen at the bottom of the page. *(fols. 83v-84v)*

[Border page: *Presentation of the Virgin*, November 21. *fol. 82*]
[Border page: *St. Ambrose*, December 7. *fol. 85*]

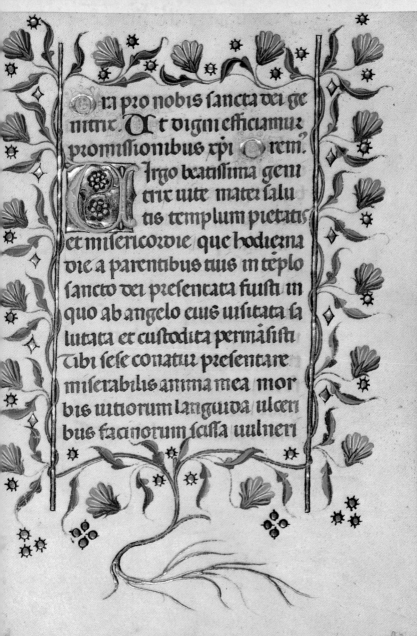

ra pro nobis sancta dei ge
nitrix. ℣t digni efficiamur
promissionibus xpi. ℟rem̄.

Irgo beatissima geni
trix uite mater salu
tis templum pietatis
et misericordie que hodierna
die a parentibus tuis in tēplo
sancto dei presentata fuisti in
quo ab angelo eius uisitata sa
lutata et custodita permāsisti
tibi sese conatur presentare
miserabilis anima mea mor
bis uitiorum languida ulceri
bus facinorum sassa uulneri

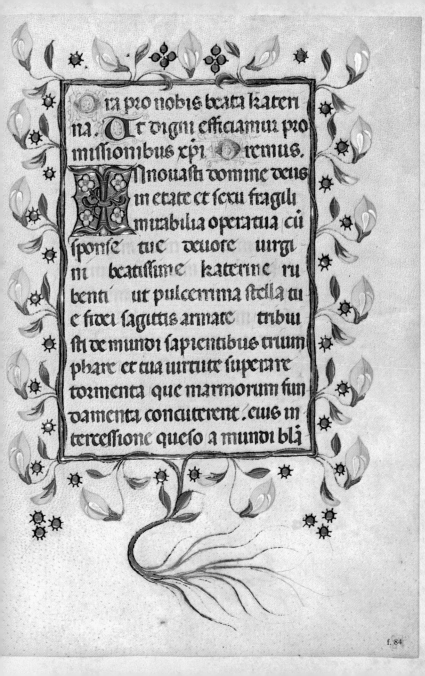

ra pro nobis beata katen
na. Et digni efficiamur pro
missionibus xpi. Oremus.

nouasti domine deus
in etate et sexu fragili
mirabilia operatua cu
sponse tue deuote uirgi
ni beatissime katerine ru
benti ut pulcerrima stella tu
e fidei sagittis armate tribui
sti de mundi sapientibus triun
phare et tua uirtute superare
tormenta que marmorum fun
damenta concuterent. eius in
tercessione queso a mundi blã

ditijs et amoribus a quibus
non debet esse timor. me ac
omnes in te confidentes tua
benignitate custodi. et sicut
in monte syna corpus ipsius
liquore mirando perfusum
mirabiliter per tuos angelos
collocasti. sic in celesti monte
me facias cum eis semper tua
martyre et uirgine katerina
pro me orante perpetua feli
citate gaudere. Qui uiuis et
regnas deus per infinita secu
la seculorum. Amen.

ora pro nobis beate ambro
sij. Ut digni efficiamur pro
missionibus xpi Oremus.
Antistitum decus ac
sanctissime doctor
Ambrosij qui ut eg
gregius pastor infulis preful
gens episcopalibus dei eccle
siam mirifice decorasti et lo
rica spiritualium virtutum
adornasti et orthodoxe fidei
contra hereticam prauitatem
clarissimus defensor fuisti.
Qui extitisti etiam sapientissi
mus in predicatione disertu

Saint Lucy

(SC̄A LUCIA VIRGO)

December 13

Saint Lucy, a virgin martyr of the early church, was denounced by a spurned suitor to the Roman governor of Syracuse, Paschasius, who ordered her death in A.D. 303. In this miniature Lucy is portrayed as a fair-haired young girl, carrying in her right hand a green book bag. She is also holding the flaming oil lamp generally associated with her. The meaning of her name in Latin, *Lucia,* is probably derived from *lux,* light. Lucy's burning lamp also links her with the wise virgins, who never let their lamps run out of oil.

The figure, draped in delicately shaded robes of pink, blue, and gray, stands on a grassy lot bordered by two rocks.

Closely spaced rows of violet flowers with five rounded petals and white centers are set against the gold background; similar blossoms with pointed petals and blank centers frame the miniature. *(fols. 89v-90v)*

[Border page: *Immaculate Conception*, December 8. *fol. 87*]
[Border page: *St. John the Evangelist*, December 27. *fol. 91-91v*]
[Border page: *St. Monica*, May 4. *fol. 93*]

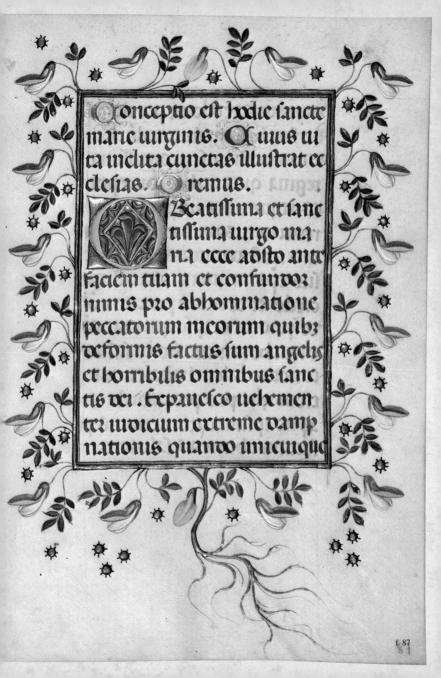

Conceptio est hodie sancte
marie virginis. Cuius vi
ta inclita cunctas illustrat ec
clesias. Oremus.

Beatissima et sanc
tissima virgo ma
ria ecce adsto ante
faciem tuam et confundor
nimis pro abhominatione
peccatorum meorum quibz
deformis factus sum angelis
et horribilis omnibus sanc
tis dei. Expauesco uehemen
ter iudicium extreme damp
nationis quando unicuique

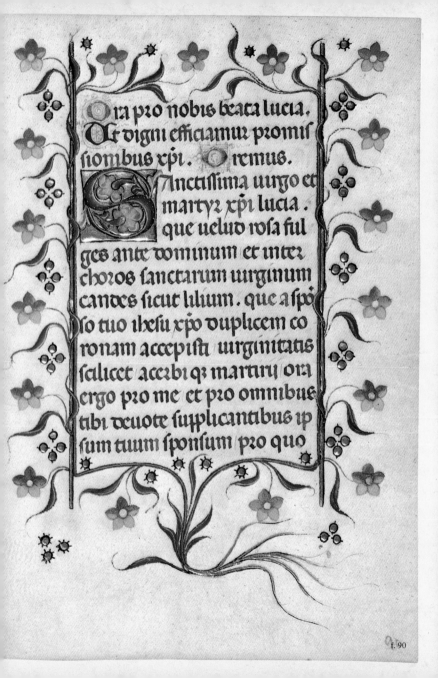

Ora pro nobis beata lucia.
Et digni efficiamur promis
sionibus xpi. Oremus.
Sanctissima uirgo et
martyr xpi lucia.
que uelud rosa ful
ges ante dominum et inter
choros sanctarum uirginum
candes sicut lilium. que a spo
so tuo ihesu xpo duplicem co
ronam accepisti uirginitatis
scilicet acerbi qz martirij ora
ergo pro me et pro omnibus
tibi deuote supplicantibus ip
sum tuum sponsum pro quo

nec minas principum nec san
guinem tuum effundere timu
isti quatenus adiutorio ipsi
us possim cuncta caduca et
transitoria displicentia qz sibi
despicere et amplecti eterna
ambulemcz fideliter sicut tu
ambulasti ut tandem perueni
am ad desideratum regnum
permansurum ad quod tu bea
tissima peruenisti . Quod michi
prestare dignetur qui te suo
amori copulauit ihesus xps
qui cum patre et spiritu sancto
est in secula benedictus. Amē .

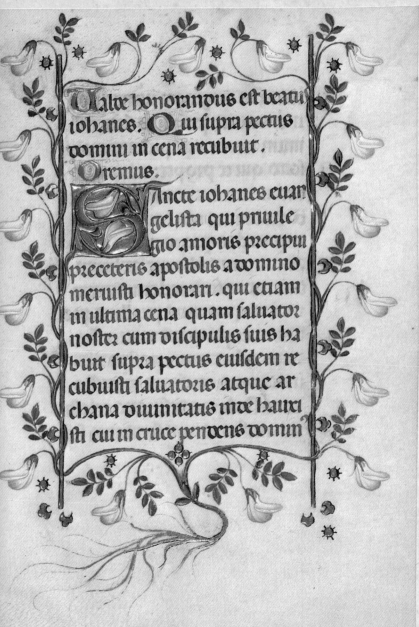

Valde honorandus est beatus
iohanes. Qui supra pectus
domini in cena recubuit.
Oremus.

Sancte iohanes euan
gelista qui priuile
gio amoris precipui
preceteris apostolis a domino
meruisti honorari. qui etiam
in ultima cena quam saluator
noster cum discipulis suis ha
buit supra pectus eiusdem re
cubuisti saluatoris atque ar
chana diuinitatis inde hauri
sti cui in cruce pendens domin

matrem uirginem uirgini co
mendauit. per illius sanctissi
mum nomen ac pietatem ob
secro qui te propter tuam casti
tatem in tantum dilexit ut hec
bona omnia tibi conferret ut
intercedas pro meis delictis
ac omnium tibi rite adheren
tium ad ipsum redemptorem
meum quatenus per illius pie
tatem et per tuam intercessio
nem delictorum nostrorum
ualeamus consequi remissio
nem. Noli me despicere celesti
um misteriorum scrutator sed

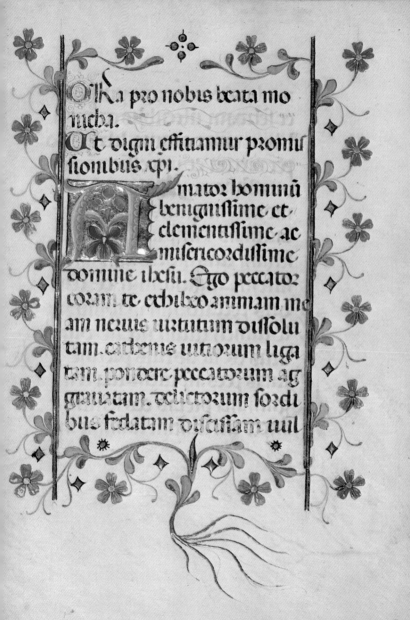

Ora pro nobis beata mo
nicha.
Ut digni efficiamur promis
sionibus xpi.

Amator hominum
benignissime et
clementissime ac
misericordissime
domine ihesu. Ego peccator
torum te echibeo animam me
am neque virtutum dissolu
tam. ac vene vitiorum liga
tam. pondere peccatorum ag
gravatam. delictorum sordi
bus fedatam disfusam vul